Finding Freedom

Steve Sherwood

Cincinnati Book Publishers

Finding Freedom

Steve Sherwood

ISBN-13: 978-0-9772720-6-8

ISBN-10: 0-9772720-6-0

Published by
Cincinnati Book Publishers
2449 Fairview Ave., Cincinnati, OH 45219
Cincinnati Book Publishers
http://www.cincybooks.com

President: Anthony W. Brunsman
Editor: Mark P. Painter
Cover design: Brent Beck
Text design: Mark P. Painter
Printed by John S. Swift Co., Inc.
Printed in the United States of America
First Edition, 2007

Finding Freedom:

The Five Choices That Will Change Your Life

Contents

Dedication

This book is dedicated to my parents, who ignited my desire for self-discovery, and to my wife Lisa who sustains me through it.

Acknowledgments

I would like to acknowledge those who have made this book possible, starting with Michael Avery, Tom Wilhite, Jim Quinn and Sue Paige, who gave me the opportunity to teach. Mike and Nancy Monahan and the team at Life Success Seminars have provided limitless opportunity to develop and refine the ideas. I would also like to thank Dan, Tony, and Mike for pushing and Jan for the right goad at the right time.

I especially thank those whose stories have inspired and taught me, Henry, Kathy, Nancy, Lidia, Deb, and all of you who have shared your life on these pages.

Finally, thanks to Sue Gilster for your encouragement, Deb and Bob for your editing, and Tony for bringing this to fruition.

Preface

Between A Rock and a Hard Place

Every day people all over the world find themselves between a rock and a hard spot. Some of them hold on, doing what they have always done until their strength gives out and they fall onto the rocks below. Other people find the capacity to do extraordinary things; leaps to freedom that they never imagined could be within their grasp. We have all heard the stories of those who were faced with the impossible, finding the strength or courage to do the incredible. Most of the stories seem to have the common ingredient of life-and-death situations. Few have learned how to harness that ability to use during their ordinary waking hours.

You may never be stuck on the side of a cliff hoping to hold on but feeling your strength giving out. You can, however, probably relate to the feeling. Maybe your "rock and a hard place" is in staying in a job or career long past the point of burnout, or perhaps you are in a relationship that you know could be worth having if you only found the strength to change.

The stories in this book are about people who have discovered five critical steps and found the freedom to do the incredible.

These pages are dedicated to unleashing that potential in you.

Introduction

"All men dream: but not equally. Those who dream by night in the dusty recesses of their minds wake in the day to find that it was vanity: But the dreamers of the day are dangerous men for they may act their dreams with open eyes to make it possible."
T.E. Lawrence

I was drawn to the possibilities in Lawrence's quote since the first time I heard it. I was one of the "vain dreamers" whose hopes were rarely acted on and my dreams were unfulfilled.

In 1974, I started on a journey that led to a life beyond anything I had ever dreamed for myself. It began simply seeking a way to overcome my shyness in social situations and a hope of being more intimate in relationships. I thought it might take a few months, maybe a year or two, and I'd be done. Then I would be ready to get on with the business of life.

I never thought this simple quest was really a search that would challenge who I assumed I was and what I thought I could achieve. I learned that as good as life was I had only touched the surface of what I was capable of achieving. During the last 30 years, I have experienced the thrill of encountering and overcoming my own limitations and leading others through the same process. I learned the critical choices required to be free from my own limitations and give my dreams the chance to become reality. I had become as in T.E. Lawrence's words, one of the "dangerous ones."

1

Freedom

There was always a feeling of something missing, or something out of place. It was as if the picture of my life that looked so complete, upon closer inspection would prove to have little unfinished gaps, places where the paint didn't quite match or the colors on top were just covering up uglier colors underneath. There seemed to be more that I wanted in life. I was always proving myself, but feeling like a fraud.

Kathy, 40-year-old school principal

Kathy, like so many of us, had an unspoken truth. There was a voice deep inside her that desperately wanted to be heard. It was a message of change, an insight about what needed to happen for her to find the sense of wholeness she had always wanted. What she hadn't yet recognized was that the voice was calling for freedom.

Most of us have such a message inside. It usually comes as a feeling of vague frustration—a voice that speaks to us during the quiet moments telling us there must be something more—that we haven't quite done what we need to be doing.

Kathy had done the best she knew; yet she still felt a longing for something else. This is how she described her life to that point:

I had what one could only call a good life, with a nice home and family all around. Friends and colleagues commented often on my unfailing smile and outgoing personality. So what could be wrong with all of this? Nothing could be said against such a life, and yet I felt that I was just waiting for something.

I had held back from taking graduate work, but with the encouragement of administrators, I got into a masters' degree program. Again, upon suggestion from others, I pursued an administrative license and then began to think of what more could be in my life. I really, though I wouldn't have said it, wanted to shine, and shine brightly. I knew, at one level, that I was a talented person (hadn't everyone been telling me that?), but there was no real inner belief in it. I couldn't allow myself to believe that. I felt as if the compliments were unfounded, the friendship offered would soon be revoked, and the career success had always to be limited. I could not take the risk to step out and ask for what I wanted in life, and so I held myself back, always waiting and hoping that someone would see what I had to offer, but secretly convinced that if I stepped out of the shadows and into the light, "they" would see the truth, that I really was not worthy. I wanted other people to see who I was and ask me to step up; I couldn't claim it for myself.

Kathy seemed destined to a life of waiting—waiting for others to see what was great inside her and to draw it out. She didn't notice this about herself and if others said it, she couldn't hear it. Kathy was blind to the limits that were constraining her talents, her potential, and the satisfaction and excitement that comes from exercising them to the fullest. In time, she heard that voice inside that had subtly urged her to wake up, to see the truth of who she really was and what she could achieve. Kathy found that if she really wanted to be fulfilled, she would first have to find freedom.

There comes a time for many of us when life as we have lived it isn't good enough. Like Kathy, we start to feel confined, hemmed in by our routines and beliefs about ourselves. The need for change often shows up in our attitudes and behaviors before we ourselves recognize what's going on. Those around us are often the first to notice that something has changed or may be changing. All too often, they start asking: "What's wrong?" They imply by the very question the common belief that change only occurs to fix an ailment or problem.

As we start to look around us for options, it can appear chaotic and confusing. Many people don't understand that they may feel an itch to change based on what's right about them, not what's wrong.

Oddly, there are clearer definitions of what may be wrong with us than there are models of what's right. Psychology has continuously refined its ability to diagnose and treat the ailments of the human psyche. With all our understanding of what can go awry with us, we seem limited in our ability to describe health. It is commonly spoken of only as the absence of identifiable problems.

This reminds me of the old story of the man who goes to the psychiatrist's office and is given the Rorschach inkblot test. When he is shown the first inkblot and asked what he sees, he responds, "I see a naked woman." The doctor shows him the second picture and he responds that he sees a naked woman. With each succeeding picture, he has the same response. When the doctor concludes that he may have a sexual obsession the man replies: "Don't blame me—*you're* the one with the dirty pictures!"

As silly as the story is, I have found that many people find themselves in the same position. When they start to feel dissatisfied or uneasy with life and begin looking for answers, they often feel that every answer they have is wrong. They may feel that every path of change starts with the premise that there is something wrong with them as a person. It may feel like that the only reason to seek change is to fix a problem. We have a hard time understanding that many people have a drive to find what more they may become, not because of what is wrong, but as a sign of what is right. The question, "What kind of problem do I have?" seems like a logical start in a society that waits to cure illness instead of preparing for health.

It still amazes me how much useless time I spent looking for what was *wrong* with me when what I needed to be doing was finding what was *next* for me. I had done the best I could with what I knew and found it no longer satisfied me. I, like Kathy, heard that vague call inside that wanted something more. I wasn't a failure; I wasn't sick; I was unfulfilled. It wasn't a call for a cure; it was a call to growth.

Too often, we have waited for life to become unmanageable before we begin to change. Though in the area of our physical health more enlightened thinking has led us to move towards preventative medicine achieved through a physically healthy lifestyle, we are only just beginning to focus on achieving a healthy interpersonal lifestyle. More and more, people are changing how they live in order to find what's best in them, rather than as a reaction to illness or pain.

During our lifetime, there has been a growing movement to find and maximize our human potential. It is a movement that isn't about going from bad to good or from sickness to health, but of finding out who we really are and what we are really capable of.

Most of us were raised in environments that taught us to live and behave in accordance with the direction of others. The average "healthy" family works hard to instill in each of us the appropriate values and ethics of the society in which we live. Learning to live within the norms of society is not only critical for the success of the society but is equally important for the individual. There comes a time, though, when we have done our best to fit into that standard and have matured in that arena. We then begin to wonder what more is available to us. This is a natural and intuitive process that arises within us. It generally is not one that is planned or even well thought-out as it occurs. Quite often, those of us who are engaged in it don't have a clue about it. We are surprised by the need to change and the chaos it can create.

Abraham Maslow addressed this in his pyramid of needs. The order of human development starts with the need to survive. It progresses with the need for security. After that has been achieved, we seek to fit into society, to belong. Self-esteem follows belonging and then, finally—and only if all the lower-level needs are met—we reach for the highest rung in the hierarchy, which Maslow calls "self-actualization." This is where we begin the work to find out who we truly are and to live our lives accordingly.

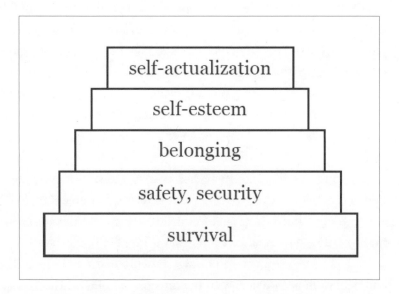

I remember studying this in my twenties and wondering, "OK—but how?" In my work with people over the last 30 years, I have slowly come to grips with what this means to me. I have also noticed that. although each of us is different, the basic process can be much the same.

During those same 30 years, the field of personal growth has blossomed. When I started, there were a handful of different processes and teachers. The community of people involved was also small and somewhat interconnected. It seemed that we all knew, or knew of, most of the people involved. Today it's a different story. There is a bewildering array of books, seminars, and teachers providing myriad opportunities to those seeking change. I am regularly asked if I know about some new process or technique. The choices are so great that it can become confusing to pick out not only the good from the bad, but also what's personally relevant.

For those beginning the process of finding freedom, it can be easy to be waylaid by the many really good pitfalls along the way. Most of us fall into at least one. There have been times when I felt I had managed to hit them all!

Everywhere there are examples of people being stuck, but relatively few examples of people who seem to have broken through to finding genuine peace, even joy, with who they really are. The stories about those who have made this journey can be invaluable inspiration to help us in our own quest. Unfortunately, they are often so personal in nature that they may give us hope as to the possibilities but no clear path that we may follow for ourselves. One person's path may look like another's rut; a stepping-stone for one may appear as a stumbling block to another.

There are, nevertheless, five critical choices that are common to those who have made this journey. Even though the specifics of the steps may be different, the *nature* of the changes is similar.

A simple way to begin is with a diagram I saw years ago. It provided an easy and understandable guide to where I was then and what I needed to do to find freedom.

Think of yourself as having three distinct layers as pictured:

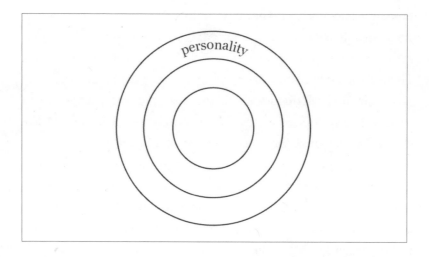

This is an overly simple but effective diagram of a person. We will start with the outside layer—the personality. I was raised knowing it was important to have a "good" personality. I had an assumption of what a personality was and would have defined it as a set of values that we show others. Webster defines it as "one's personal characteristics." Over the years of my work, I've asked hundreds of people how they define it. The most common answers I hear are "It's who we are" or "It's how we show ourselves to others."

Interestingly, the root of the word comes from the Greek word "Persona." Even though we get the word person from this root, that isn't what it means. It literally translates to "mask." Think back to when you were told it was important to have a good personality. What they were actually telling you was that you should wear a good mask. Why? Are we, like the Phantom of the opera, somehow deformed and unfit for society?

Perhaps it is only because society works better when people adopt certain roles and follow common rules. Regardless of *why* we wear masks, the fact is that we learn from an early age to cover our "selves." We cover many of our true thoughts and feelings from each other and in many cases, from ourselves. We often find ourselves pretending to be different from how we really are.

Sometimes this is done out of politeness to others—at other times, out of fear of being known.

The path of freedom is one of setting aside the mask and finding out *who* has been wearing it. Unfortunately, some of us have worn our mask for so long that we no longer see it as a mask. We truly believe in our own deception.

Think for a moment of how you cover your thoughts and feelings. My friend Nancy (who you will hear more from in a later chapter) says that she regularly uses humor to ease tense situations. She also notices that she will smile at people who have hurt her feelings as if to say, "Its okay; I don't mind." She regularly tells jokes to hide her own embarrassment. She does the same thing whether she is receiving compliments or criticism.

Just as Nancy uses humor, I know of people who mask with hostility, sarcasm, thoughtfulness, and even spirituality—ironically hiding behind personal growth, using the arcane jargon that comes with it to cover what they really fear about themselves. Each of us has a slightly different way of shielding our thoughts and feelings but the result is the same. Who we *are* remains a mystery. The mystery of who we really are isn't confined to others not knowing us. The mystery of why we do what we do, of what really drives us, is often as confounding to us as it is to others.

This may not matter much at work or in casual relating, but it all too often carries over into our most important relationships. Many times, I have talked in depth with men and women who are contemplating leaving a marriage or long-term relationship. When asked why they are leaving, they often respond that they can't really put it into words. When I ask them what their partner thinks, they tell me they haven't told them yet. Their most important thoughts and feelings regarding the relationship are kept secret from the person who needs to know them most!

As tragic as this lack of communication is, the departing person frequently doesn't really know why they are dissatisfied. She may not know what she really wants; all she knows is that she is unfulfilled and thinks that maybe a change of partners will "fix" it. Predictably, most people take their problems with them to their next partner and end up in the same place with the new relationship.

Until they take off the mask and explore their own inner territory, the results will end up much the same.

This brings us to the second layer—the Shadow. Under the skin of personality lie parts of us that we are vaguely familiar with, but that we are reluctant to look at completely, or for too long. In this layer are trapped unresolved feelings and unexamined self-limiting beliefs.

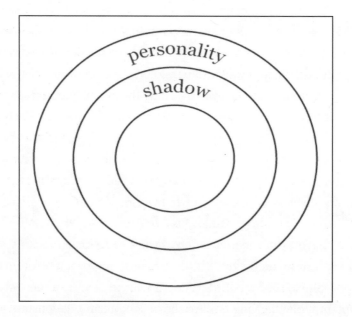

The unresolved feelings are the leftover emotional fragments from events that we didn't have the means or desire to deal with at the time of the event. For one person, it may have been a death of a loved one that was never fully grieved; for another, it may be a feeling of never being quite good enough. Many times, I have heard stories of broken homes or marriages that have left a well of sadness in someone, with no known way to release it.

It is impossible to make it through life without tragedy. It is also rare to know how to deal fully with the tragedy when it comes. Most often, people "stuff" the feelings they don't know how to release. They convince themselves that the pain will dissipate in time. Until that time, they will put on a happy face and "tough it out."

I had a friend who used to refer to this as proud flesh. We were both raised in Arizona, and he was familiar with the term from keeping livestock in corrals. When a horse is kept in a corral and has an itch, it will scratch itself by rubbing on a fence post. This will occasionally result in splinters. When a horse gets a splinter it may try to bite it out or rub it out on another fence post. This can break the splinter off under the skin. In time, the skin will heal over the broken splinter. The horse may look fine but there is a wound under the surface that is slowly festering.

We are the same way. At various times we have been wounded in the heart. We have healed over the wound so we may appear to be fine, but the problem has only been hidden by our mask—not resolved. When someone tries to ride that horse, everything will be fine until he touches that wounded spot. When that happens, he is thrown and the horse runs off.

The same behavior happens between people. When someone touches a hidden wounded spot, they can cause pain without knowing how or why. The wounded person may not even know why, but will respond in much the same way as that horse—putting as much distance as possible between themselves and whoever touched that wound. Unfortunately, this is often the person who is closest to us, the one we let close enough to touch our heart.

The feelings *don't* dissipate in time, but continue to be a source of pain. It is a curious thing about the emotions that we stuff. Rather than lessening, they often grow, and can grow out of proportion to the initial event. The more we repress them, the stronger the urge to release them becomes.

Ultimately, we end up using an incredible amount of our energy in silently protecting ourselves from letting out those uncomfortable expressions. We then wonder what has happened to the joy and enthusiasm we used to feel. What we don't notice is how much energy we are using to carry our baggage. Life can be difficult enough just dealing with the day-to-day events we encounter; if we are carrying a load of unresolved baggage, it can become unbearable. Yet we do carry it, now too familiar with the burden to even regard it as abnormal. If we, like Kathy, can also manage to smile often and get a lot done, our world conspires with us to encourage us to stay where we are.

This is so difficult for us to recognize because we are usually unaware that we are stuffing feelings at the time it happens. Most of us have become so adept at it that we can hide our feelings before we are even aware that we have them. And there are so many others around us acting in the same manner that we come to believe it's the normal and proper way to be.

This task of letting go of these emotional remnants is best accomplished with outside guidance. Most of us find it relatively easy to fool ourselves about the work we need to do, and skilled guidance can accelerate our progress. There are some excellent intensive workshops that can assist in uncovering and dealing with those remnants.* For some, the severity of the issues necessitates a more traditional therapeutic approach. We are amazingly resilient as people; there are situations, however, that are best handled with professional counseling.

I cannot emphasize enough the importance of doing this work. I have met hundreds of people who want to get on with fulfilling their dreams and yet seem to be incapable of making them come true. It is often the case that they are carrying the weight of past baggage and it has become so familiar that it seems effortless. It has

---

* See http://www.lifesuccessseminars.com for an author-recommended and established resource.

become so normal to carry the weight that it is hard to believe that it even exists. Yet each day they are using so much of their energy and vitality that they don't have enough left to accomplish their really important dreams.

The unresolved issues often tie directly to the second area of shadow—your self-limiting beliefs. To ignore the importance of the feelings while trying to clear out the beliefs can be a futile act that leads only to frustration. It is important that you be emotionally ready and energized before continuing. We are often taught, either directly or through the school of life, that there are some things that are beyond us. This may be true in some cases. For example, I will never play professional basketball, having neither the size nor the talent. There are some things that we don't have the gifts or the aptitudes to achieve. But in many cases, it is only the *belief* that we can't have or do something that holds us back.

I remember hearing a story attributed to the great escape artist, Houdini. In the story, Houdini was asked to test the security of a new "inescapable" jail cell. Upon arrival, Houdini was frisked at the door and then left alone inside as the massive door shut.

Once inside he started to work, using some cleverly hidden lock picks. He gently placed his ear against the lock in order to hear the slightest movement of the tumblers. In the beginning, he worked full of confidence that this lock, like all the others, wouldn't be a challenge.

As time passed and he made no progress, he became increasingly worried. As his allotted time expired and he hadn't gotten the first tumbler to click, he collapsed against the door in defeat, at which point his weight pushed it open! Only then did he realize that after the door was shut someone had forgotten to lock it. *He had been imprisoned only by his own belief.*

You see everywhere around you people living that story right now. They are living confined within a jail cell they believe to be locked. They think someone or some circumstance has placed limits on what they can do, or be, or achieve. They may also believe that someone else holds the key to their release. Many people act as if the limits that hold them back are insurmountable and believe that there is no sense in making the attempt. Yet we are all aware of the extraordinary obstacles that some people have overcome. We are surrounded with examples of those who have excelled despite physical handicaps, prejudice, social injustice, and any number of seemingly unscalable obstacles. It is too easy to convince ourselves that those people who have done this are somehow "different" than us. We think they must have some special or unique character, when in actuality, the unique feature they have is the will to begin. The good fortune to find the appropriate technique comes to those who first find the will to try.

People often use the excuse: "I don't know how to start." But, though the path may be obscure, once you've begun it you will notice that the signs have been there all along. Each of us is receiving innumerable notices from our unconscious minds and the world around us telling us where and how to start. Ultimately, the biggest barrier to starting is fear—fear that once we open the door into the unknown part of ourselves, a whole host of new and unknown parts of ourselves could be discovered. "What if I am worse than I thought?" "What if I can't handle what I find?"

Several years ago. Larry Niven and Jerry Pournelle undertook the challenge of doing a liberal update of Dante's Inferno. They called this new version simply "Inferno," and in it, the main character wakes up one day realizing that somehow he has died and is in hell. This hell isn't like the hell of his imagination, a place of fiery pits and devilish creatures. This hell is a dry, dusty desert town where nothing grows and the people are aloof and distant. He can see—way off in the distance—the outer wall of this prison and decides to hike out to the wall and see if he can find a way out. What he discovers is that no matter how long he walks toward that wall, he never gets closer. It stays always within his sight, but beyond his grasp. After a while, he finds a man who says he can guide him out. The guide tells him that to walk toward the wall is useless—that he can never escape in that way. The only hope of escape lies in going away from the wall and deeper inside, to the very center of hell. The guide also tells him that the journey will take him through all the horrors that he imagined hell could be, and that it will be a long and sometimes terrifying journey. The journey will be painful and will test his will and his resolve.

This story is universally true in at least one way; we can't escape ourselves by getting away from our center. We do have to go through the parts of ourselves that we fear and it *will* be a test of our resolve. We may find out that there are parts of us that we don't like or that we are uncomfortable with. Whether we like it or not, ultimately we all have to face our own internal demons if we want to be free.

Fortunately, most of us don't find it to be a hellish journey full of *only* pain, or beyond our endurance. The greatest obstacle is facing the fear of getting started; you *do* have the strength to face yourself and to pass the test. Where some seem to fall short is in finding the courage to begin.

Fear "What you fear appears"

I often hear this quote, although I don't know who said it first. I suppose on one level it's very true. Those who perpetually live in fear are constantly confronted with the specter of fear. They see proof to justify their fear everywhere. It is always with them. They may also help grow those fears by feeding them constant focus and attention. For example, as a teen, I so feared rejection from girls that I became even more self-conscious and tongue-tied while asking them out for dates, thus guaranteeing what I feared most.

For most of us, the majority of our fears are most apparent in the effect that the resulting stress creates in us. On those occasions when we do encounter the objects of our fears, they often aren't as difficult as we had imagined. Only occasionally are they as bad as or worse than we thought.

A case in point: my wife Lisa is a fanatical animal lover. In particular, she loves dogs. She is constantly rescuing strays and watching out for those dogs that live in the neighborhood.

She has a great fondness for Buddy, the golden retriever next door. She is always bringing him treats and is concerned for his safety. She worries about him nightly, afraid that there are "wild dogs" that live in the nearby woods who will do him harm.

Any time she hears strange dog sounds at night she will jump up and check through the window to make sure that Buddy is ok. Recently she heard what sounded like dogs barking next door. Though it was 4:00 am, she hopped out of bed to check on his safety.

When she got to the window, I heard her cry out that someone's puppies had gotten out. With that, she went running down the stairs and out the front door. Still half asleep, I dragged myself out of bed, not sure what the problem was. Were we saving stray puppies, or rescuing Buddy from a pack of wild dogs? And if the latter, would Lisa herself now need rescuing?

As it turned out, her worst fear *had* come true. When she came out of the house, Buddy *was* surrounded by a pack of wild dogs. When Lisa arrived, the wild pack turned their attention on her. What she feared had appeared. The leader of this "pack of beasts" was a Chihuahua. As the alpha male, he was the largest and fiercest of the lot. His pack had originally descended from wolves and was no doubt still driven by those same instincts. Buddy was so "concerned" that he was wagging his tail. Having sized up Lisa, the pack took off and hid under some bushes. Worried still that they might be someone's lost dogs, Lisa waited until they came back out. They appeared once more, began yapping excitedly, and disappeared back into the woods.

As happened with Lisa, many times when what we fear does appear, we find that the worst part of it was the anticipation. How often in your life have you had to face one of your fears only to find that the dragon you were anticipating was in reality a pack of wild puppies? We often develop our fears at an age or time of life when we aren't very strong or capable. We hold onto the fear even after our talents and abilities have changed. We still think we will have to somehow measure up to the fear as we were then, not as we are now.

I have heard that in India they train young elephants to stay by tying them to a post with rope. As an infant, the elephant can't break the rope. When they are older, the elephants still think the rope is stronger even though the elephant could easily break it. The elephants still relate to that rope as if it were weak, just as we relate to our fears as if we were incapable.

For those who find the courage and face the challenge of going through the shadow, the reward comes from arriving at the center. This is the essence of who we are. This is where we get to find the person we are, using the talents and gifts that we were born with to their fullest. This is also the hardest to describe in that it is personal to each of us.

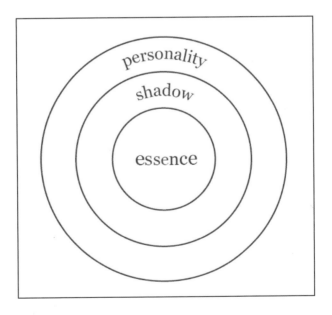

There is no quick fix. We have many years invested in maintaining our limits. The tenacity and strength of intention that has us holding onto these limits requires an equal level of commitment to break free. The people who will share their stories and triumphs in the following pages have spent years of their lives working to win their freedom. Anyone believing that a "once-over" of the concepts and practices in this book will be sufficient for change is seeking the easy way out. The process of uncovering the true self is a lifelong journey.

For those who have the desire and the will to follow through, there is the gift of freedom waiting inside. Initially this freedom is a release from the emotional baggage and the constraints of what we have been taught about ourselves. In time, it gets even better. In each of us there are gifts left unexplored. This is so because they are contrary to who we *think* we are or because they don't fit with our model of how we *should* behave.

There is such an incredible feeling of lightness and exuberance in releasing our baggage that many people stop at that. They think that now that they feel better, they have grown or changed in some important way. They believe that the happiness will last and that they have learned what they need to know. Those people will ultimately find themselves slowly losing their excitement, however, as they continue the same behaviors that created the baggage in the first place.

Real change is more than just letting go of the past. Change truly becomes meaningful when you find the freedom to discover the hidden gifts and strengths that have laid dormant inside. Many of us think we know who we are. But often what we really know is who we have been. You may find that you have believed your image of yourself and have missed what lays undiscovered in the depth.

In casting off the mantle of who you have pretended to be, you will find a new sense of purpose—one that has been hinted at by the gifts and talents you were born with, but which has never been fully revealed.

As you start to explore who you really are and what you are truly capable of, you will experience a deep sense of pleasure with how you live and an ease with "living in your own skin." Some people who are beginning this voyage may be hoping to find a constant "high" of happiness. Others hope to escape the sad and tragic events in life. There will still be sad days and hard times. The difference will be in how you feel about yourself as you go through them, how you now learn from and even appreciate them as part of life, and how quickly you let them pass on.

There are five critical choices that must be made to complete this journey. They are gates that must be passed through, and best done in order. These choices serve as a foundation on which to build a different life—the life most people think is beyond them. Some of these choices may *sound* familiar, and you may be tempted to skim over those sections. Here, however, you will find them presented with a different twist. For your quest for clarity and freedom to be truly effective, it is important not only to understand these choices as stated, but also to understand them within the framework presented in the following pages.

The First Choice of Freedom

2

The Search for Understanding

"The unexamined life is one not worth living." Socrates

Over two thousand years ago, the quest of Socrates was much the same as ours is today: to know oneself. The challenge is that who we really are is often hidden from us. We are better at seeing who we *think* we are and who we think we *should* be. There exists in each of us, however, a truth that is unknown and so remains unspoken. These truths have dramatic impact on our lives and our fortunes, yet for too many of us, they are never uncovered.

Kathy, the school principal from the first chapter, lived a life that she believed would bring satisfaction. She had learned values and principles that were supposed to lead her to fulfillment. She was a dedicated teacher, a thoughtful and loving partner and wife, and an inspiring mother. She lived a good life, a life that she was raised believing should have been enough, yet she felt the need to do more.

Each time those yearnings would arise she would respond in

the same way—she would do more of what she was already doing. She would take on more projects and exceed other's expectations; she would give more to her family and classroom. Yet this was never enough to quiet the voice inside. Kathy could never do enough to ease those yearnings.

Kathy had learned a formula for living that didn't fully satisfy her real needs as a person. There was nothing wrong with what she was doing; most of it was valuable to her and the community in which she lived. It was the unspoken needs that she wasn't satisfying. Unfortunately, each time she felt the unconscious urge to change she would respond by doing what she already did, only a little bit more. It seemed as if happiness lay in doing what she was already doing faster or harder or more often.

This continued to impress and bring recognition from others, which made it rewarding enough to continue. Unfortunately, it also kept her so busy that she had neither the time nor the energy to truly examine her life. She couldn't realize that what she needed was to slow down and reevaluate what she thought would bring happiness.

It finally struck her that more wasn't better. She had spent her life trying her best with a formula that wasn't ever going to succeed. It was time to know herself. It was time to listen to the voice within, to find the unspoken truth.

Her search, like so many before it, started with the question: *"Why? Why am I in this situation? How have I come to be like this?"*

The First Choice of Freedom

Since the time of Socrates, many of humanity's greatest minds have written volumes about how we have come to be the way we are. For many years, it was thought that fate or God's will determined who we were and how our lives would turn out. With the coming of the scientific age, the debate began around nature vs. nurture. Were we born with a biological blueprint for our personality or are we a product of our upbringing and environment? Genetic scientists continue to plumb the depths of our genetic code, searching in part for clues to the nature of our personality. Is it in our genes? Are there genetic factors that determine aspects of our character and personality? If so, then what percent do genes alone explain?

Social scientists examine the impact of family structure, the influence of early childhood experience, and of significant lifetime events. Others still prefer to believe in fate or destiny.

It's not my place to argue the merits or the amount of influence of any of these factors. In 30 years of working with people to help them change the way they live their lives, it has become apparent to me that there is interplay of all three.

It appears that we are born with separate and distinct aspects of character. Babies, even identical twins, will respond to the same circumstances in their own individual and unique way. If you have had children, you probably have noticed that your children had different ways of acting at birth. Some were easygoing, others very demanding; some are shy and others bold; they were different in many ways. Children are not blank slates at birth, waiting to be programmed into the child of our wishes. We have to work with who's already there at birth.

One of the most popular topics on daytime TV is what happens when parents don't respect the innate nature of their children and attempt to mold them into something else. For several hours a day we can listen to the hardships of those whose parents or family tried to program them into a person they were not. Even more disturbing are the stories of outright abuse and neglect. These are huge factors influencing our personalities. By themselves, though, these can't completely account for the uniqueness of us as individuals. I have worked with people who were raised by ignorant or outright abusive parents who turned out very differently than their upbringing would suggest.

There is a common perception that we, like computers, are

programmable, that an instruction repeated often enough and with enough force will become a program that will be followed. Parents, on the other hand, often feel that nothing they say is taken to heart or acted upon. How many of us have heard our parents say, "If I've told you once, I've told you a thousand times!" as we were growing up? Our parents were doing their best to help us learn values and life skills that would become the foundation for success in our future relationships and careers.

We, on the other hand, were doing our best to do what was most fulfilling to us in the moment. Parents' perspectives, gained from years of their own experiences, felt like constraints to us. We demanded to make the very mistakes that they were trying to protect us from. Most parents are involved in the same effort with their children, and unfortunately, they occasionally cross the line. They attempt to create in their children the person they wish they could be, denying who they actually are. They place constraints—not to nurture, but ones that become limits or barriers to growth and maturation. Many of these children have grown up feeling the effects of these "programs" that did set in.

Some children do live what they learn. Many children raised with judgment learn to condemn, or those raised with love learn to love, and some raised with abuse become abusers. Programs are certainly an important influence on how we behave, but they fall short of completely explaining how we turn out. One of the most powerful examples I have encountered of this is the story of Henry. He was ruthlessly programmed to hide not only his feelings but also his history, ethnicity, and his body as well.

Amsterdam 1940—The Nazi Occupation

"Go hinter!" "Go in there!" My grandmother became impatient. She picked me up and shoved me into the closet and told me to be quiet. I think at that point I got it. I was really scared, mostly for her. I heard from neighbors that things happened when

people were taken. I remember thinking I would be invisible. I stayed as quiet as I could. I noticed how loud my breathing was. I felt like I had to be a statue. I heard steps. There I was, about to lose my grandmother, and I could do nothing but be silent. I couldn't cry or protest or whimper or do any God damn thing. I just let it happen.

This is one of the most vivid memories of my early childhood. We had been living in Amsterdam four or five months before the Germans came. We were in a Jewish neighborhood. I was about 4 years old when I started to see their trucks on the streets. Sometimes I saw them full of people wearing yellow stars like me. We constantly heard the sound of boots and the banging on the door as people pleaded not to be taken. We would hold our breath until they left. One day they came to our door. Grandmother said to hide; I said no. I would be with her. She held her finger to her lips: "Shhhhh!" I was to be silent. She picked me up and put me in the closet; it didn't seem that she was strong enough to lift me, but she did. The last I saw of her was her finger to her lips "Sshhhhh!" admonishing me to be silent.

I never saw her again.

I felt a sense of betrayal that "she wouldn't take me with her." I took it as she didn't want me anymore. I decided, "If you don't want me I won't go with you. I won't get caught; I will stay hidden and I will be a statue." It wasn't my fear of being caught; I didn't then know what really happened—it was more a hiding from rejection. I will be invisible to save myself from hurt. I stayed for an eternity until neighbors came to check. I remember my mother coming home and being thankful for me but she was very scared; we didn't know what would happen next. We left with little and stayed on the move for the next three months, staying a night or two here or there in basements and attics.

Friesland 1942

We found our way to a farm and she told me we would go into hiding. At the last moment she said we would be apart; she told me we wouldn't hide together. I never thought my mother would separate us. I was furious at first, then I felt myself as if I was melting. I pleaded with her and she wouldn't relent so I promised I'd be good. I'd be a good boy because I thought she was punishing me for being bad. I remember turning my back to her because I was angry and feeling unforgiven and knowing I was bad. I didn't see it as saving my life. I felt it as punishment. I would be in her way, and she was leaving me.

I was taken to a small farm where there were eight children, two of us who were in hiding. Eos, who was from Holland, was blonde and blue-eyed and got to stay in school. I looked Semitic and had to stay hidden. The farm was poor, and I spent my days helping with the chores during the day and sleeping in a closet bed at night. I felt I had to be very quiet and I didn't want anyone getting pissed at me. I had to be good, and I really felt insecure and wondering would they keep me? They bleached my hair, changed my name to Hans. I was told it would be dangerous to go to school. They showed me hiding places. When the Germans were around, we would go out in the fields or hide in the potato cellar. The cellar became a familiar place. Sometimes I stayed so long I pissed in my pants. We'd do chores in the morning and I learned Dutch and Fries but didn't get any schooling until after the war. I felt like a chameleon, which no one who knows me today would say is true.

Many years after the war I asked Eos what I was like as a child. He said I was silent and watchful, withdrawn. I had to be watchful. Ours was the first house off the main road so I was always careful. I would notice the speed of vehicles. Were they going by fast or were they slow—roaming, searching.

I felt safe in the hayloft and in the open field where I could see what was coming. I was always conscious of finding a place I could go if something happened. I was always cued by the people I was with. My foster father was very astute at noticing danger and the other children, without knowing why, would take up the warning "Hans Go Go."

If we were programmable like computers, Henry would still be hidden today. One of the miracles about being human is that it doesn't necessarily work that way. We, as people in the face of extraordinary challenges, still have a say in how we turn out. I have talked to literally hundreds of people abused physically and emotionally who triumphed by not passing along the abuse. They were certainly affected by the events and have struggled to come to grips with them, but they didn't surrender to the circumstance of their upbringing.

I have known Henry for 17 years. I have been aware of his childhood and the years he spent in hiding. I can only imagine the effect that would have had on his personality as he grew. Henry has vivid memories of when and how he was told to hide. His security, and more important to him, his emotional well-being were tied up in being invisible. For eight years he practiced invisibility. Today Henry is one of the most visible people I know. He has a reputation for being very outspoken and confrontational. Something inside him wouldn't tolerate a life spent in the shadows. He started to take control back from his early learning of being hidden shortly after arriving in America.

I have also met with people who had delightful childhoods, and were raised in supportive, loving families, who now seem incapable of loving themselves or of making choices that would support feelings of self-respect or self-esteem. All too often, those in this position are looking at their lives and asking, *"Why? Why me? Who or what is the cause of my problem?"*

It is far easier to see how we suffer for our issues than how we ourselves may have had a hand in their creation. Usually we pay attention only to the circumstances of our lives, our natures at birth and the kindness or coldness of our rearing. We are also well aware of the accidents or windfalls that arrive out of the blue. After taking into account our nature at birth and acknowledging the effect of our upbringing, family structure and the seeming random acts of fate or accidents that have happened, what's left?

Choice

What's left is choice. We make choices about our future and the way we want to be. We make choices about how to handle events in our lives. We make decisions about what the circumstances in our lives mean and what we will become as a result. We often make these choices without realizing we made them. We rarely recognize the choices we've made, only the consequences when they show up. The power and influence of our unconscious choices is poorly understood, yet have an immense ability to impact our future. To allow this work to begin requires a different understanding of what choice is and, especially, a new concept of what intention is.

Choice, as it's commonly understood, is the simple act of picking between options. Would I rather have fish or pizza for dinner? Should I go to Canada or Mexico for vacation? We are faced with hundreds of choices each day—so many choices in fact that we have learned to make most of them without a moment's conscious thought. These are the ordinary decisions that each of us makes each day.

For the most part, we make these choices easily. We feel free to pick from the wide range of options that life presents. Occasionally, however, we run into a choice that, for reasons beyond our understanding, we don't have the freedom to make. How often have you, or someone you know, tried to make lifestyle changes such as to become more assertive, stop procrastinating, get organized, stick to a healthy food plan, or go on an exercise program that never materialized?

I know people who have tried to change seemingly simple

behavior dozens of times without success. Each time they feel they have more resolve but achieve the same result. They notice other people making the very changes that for them seem impossible to make. They try logic, guilt, anger, support groups, and reading self-help books, but nothing seems to work. Choice, as we commonly understand it, has failed us in these instances.

We are not always as free to choose between options that seem easy to others. Many times this ends as a frustrating spiral of failure and the resulting loss of self-esteem that goes with it. The decision seems simple, but we seem to be incapable of action. We don't stick with the food plan, get organized, maintain the exercise regime, or become assertive. It is easy to assume that these choices are beyond our means to achieve. The *real* problem, however, is that there are overriding choices we've already made—and we don't even know that we've made them!

What often lies at the heart of the issue is the fact that, in one of our more unconscious moments, we already made our decision about this matter. Our choice is already made and we don't know it. Further, we made this choice at such a deep level and with such intensity that our current wish to change doesn't have the power to undo it.

Choices made from the core of our being become intentions that are the foundation of our experience. Most often, I hear the word "intention" used to describe a conscious process that underlies our behavior. I will use it here to describe a much deeper and more potent force. These intentions are the most powerful forces at work in determining the outcome of our lives. They can assist or inhibit the achievement of our desires while remaining unknown to us consciously.

The answer to *"Why am I like this?"* is different than we usually suspect. The search often begins with an underlying theme of "Who *made* me be like this?" A successful quest for answers may start as a search for blame, but needs to end as a statement of responsibility. The best answer to *"Why am I like this?"* is *"I am not a victim."*

This is the first critical choice of freedom. It is in this moment, when I choose responsibility over victimhood, that I take back the reins and again am in control—when I understand that, given the circumstances of my life, I *decided* how I would be. I have decided from childhood what I would make of myself. The world, with all of its opportunities and misfortunes, has tried to direct me, but ultimately I choose who I become.

This is not an attempt to deny the powerful influence that family and society play on our development. They have a profound impact, and I'm not absolving them of responsibility for the part they play. In the end, however, each of us must take a stand and claim our results, regardless of the influence of outside forces. Some children live what they learn; others decide to learn how to live.

A Conversation with Henry on Being Hidden

Q: I am curious about when you decided to come out of hiding. No one I know of would consider you to be "in hiding." You described yourself professionally as a "get in face." These behaviors as a child would have been your undoing, threatening your very survival. When did this change? What were you like as a child?

A: The last question that you asked me remained a puzzlement for me after we parted on Saturday morning: "Where and when did you decide to stop hiding?" I was an instant behavior problem when I was in school. I started in the 4th grade, and I think because the teacher could speak some German I was 11 in a class of 9 year olds. We —you and I—began to explore my decision to become some sort of a mental-health professional, and that certainly was a significant contribution in helping me to move more to the fore. But it also came to me that sometime during my college years, about 1954, I participated in the school's Intramural program. I boxed. Well, I was pretty successful to the degree that the coach, Yustin Zirutis, invited me to try out for the varsity boxing team. I feel that my "doing well" was a beginning of openly expressing my feelings, particularly my anger. At that time I certainly didn't connect this to my hidden, pent-up emotions that up to then were pretty much kept in check. Although I did pretty well (13–3), my father put a stop to it about 1956. But after this I proudly wore a boxing-team jacket, joined a fraternity, ran for student government, got a Jewish girlfriend from the neighborhood whom I stole from a friend (on a dare). I became less isolated, more alive in many areas of my young adulthood.

Henry's story is unusual in the intensity of his circumstances, but the process of choice is the same. The answer to Henry's *"Why am I like this?"* is that it was the best decision he could make at the time. Life had been incredibly cruel to him; the Nazis had done their best to take from him his identity, his family, his culture, and his life. This was not Henry's choice. We don't get to choose the events and situations that occur. Nor do I mean to minimize the impact of the events in his life or to lessen the responsibilities of those who took his family from him. Despite their best efforts, however, he has stood tall and said, *"I am not a victim. I will not give in to the circumstances of my life!"* Henry has had an extraordinary life and his story is not commonplace. I know there is something unique and special in him that enabled him to rise above what another might have chosen.

That unique and special something is the will to decide what you will become despite the circumstances of your upbringing; and it is available to each of us. Many people who had similar experiences gave in to a life of despair or revenge. They surrendered not only what was taken by force but also their ability to do something about it. They have become victims of life, for life. It is tragic enough to have something precious taken by an abusive person, but to then surrender the rest of one's life to that same person adds the final insult to the initial injury. Too often, we think we *have* no choice, that our only option is to blame and to seek the "comfort" that comes with it.

I sometimes meet people who *say* that they are who they are because of the choices they made. They have the *language* of choice but not the *understanding* of choice. After agreeing that their choices are the drivers of their lives, they then want to know: *"What made me choose that?"* They don't understand that our choices are an act of free will, that "to choose" means that nothing *makes us* choose. There is a seemingly irresistible pull to seek an external cause and effect for our actions. We are desperate to believe that something causes us to do things that are beyond our control.

It is difficult to truly understand free will when we have been raised to think in terms of "cause and effect." There are often many seemingly good reasons to live life a certain way. We may have the support and understanding of everyone we know to do things (or to *not* do things) or to have beliefs that only bring us grief or limitations.

Imagine the tremendous effect Henry's early years had on him. There was an incredible pull to give in, to stay hidden, and to seek revenge. Henry has had the courage and awareness to pull himself free from his past—to learn from it, to teach others about it, but not to be controlled by it. Henry has been a pillar of the therapeutic community for 40 years.

He could have given in, surrendering his life to staying hidden, or blaming his oppressors for his inability to live a different life. His early life certainly would have been different had he been born in a different time and place.

The rules that apply to Henry's journey and the incredible obstacles he faced apply to each of us as well. Each of us must learn that ultimately we are not victims. We had no choice as to the events that occurred to us; how we have turned out, however, is based on *what we decided to do* about the circumstances we faced, not *because of* the circumstances. The first choice of freedom is responsibility. It is to truly understand the part you have played in deciding how you would be in the face of the circumstances of your life.

This brings us back to Kathy and the question of why she was the way she was. She discovered that she had made a choice. She had made it with such passion that she had stuck with it all those years. She had agreed that she was only worthwhile, that she was only truly worthy, when she was achieving goals for someone else.

When Kathy became aware of this, she uncovered the first choice of freedom. Kathy realized that she was no longer a victim. She was no longer destined to wait for others to recognize what was best in her; she had found it for herself.

Things to remember:

1. We may not get to control the circumstances that happen to us but we do get to choose how we respond to them.

2. To regain our freedom we must claim our responsibility for who we have chosen to be, despite our circumstances.

3

The Power of Intention

One of the foundations of personal development work is in understanding the power of intention. As you can see, I use intention here not in a casual way, but to describe a deeper, more potent force. It is in essence the ability to shape our experience by using the force of our will. It is a largely unconscious drive that makes our life experience fit into a familiar pattern that somehow fits us. We rarely recognize it in the moments it happens, but it can be seen over time in the recurring patterns that show up in our life.

Think for a moment of the patterns that have consistently played themselves out in your life. I remember, for instance, thinking as a teenager that I wasn't a very feeling person. I felt moderate amounts of affection or aggravation but no real passion. I thought that was just the way I was made. I thought some of us were thoughtful, analytical people and others were cursed to be driven by illogical and seemingly irrational emotions. I felt fortunate to be one of the thoughtful ones but I secretly wished I could feel passionate and heartfelt feelings. It was during the course of a seminar on early experience that I remembered an incident that had a profound effect on me.

When I was very young, my brothers and I would wait until our parents were in bed to begin an evening of mischief. The routine was always the same. We would start by playing, then wrestling, then fighting. We were completely oblivious to the slumbering giants in the next room until, aroused by the noise, my dad would come in, angry at the noise and the disregard for his sleep. This went on for a couple of years. Each time the intensity of his anger would increase as we continued to ignore his needs.

Things continued to get worse until one night when he had had enough. He was furious and towered over me in rage. I remember him telling me to go, to pack my things and leave. I felt completely helpless. Part of me was trying to figure out what to do; I had no bag, or idea how to start or where to go. I stood confused and scared until I'd had enough of being confused and scared. While standing in front of his wrath, I remember an incredible surge of surety came through me, and in that sureness, I made a promise. I swore I would never be like *that*. I would never treat someone with such anger. In words unbidden by me, I made a promise that would direct my actions for years to come. I would never be that angry with anyone. I didn't think about it again. I just stopped having big feelings. They were too dangerous. This wasn't a carefully considered or conscious decision. It wasn't something that I had analyzed. It was a spontaneous and deeply-made promise. It felt like something that rose up in me unbidden by my own thought. This is how intention usually operates.

When I first realized the impact of this incident, I couldn't wait to tell my dad. I thought that the power the story had on my life was based on what he had done, not on what I had decided to do. I was focused on him and his part in the story. I wanted him to realize the mistake he had made, not that I had any hand in what had happened. I wasn't ready to accept that responsibility and the power that comes with it. I was still looking for someone or something outside of me to blame. I thought that he had made me the way I was and should pay the consequences.

I realized later that it was I who had made me change—not him. In the face of rage, I had decided how I would be. I wouldn't have any strong anger myself. It was a decision that haunted me for years, yet it was my own doing. I had decided to give up passion because the intensity that came with it scared me. Had I been more responsible at the time, I could have come to a different promise. I might have promised to be more considerate of my father, but I wasn't ready.

It was also a rare chance to see intention operate. All too often, these decisions are made and not remembered. Sometimes they are made over such a long period of time and so subtly that they aren't ever noticed. Whether remembered or noticed or not, they have the power to rule my actions and direct the course of my life.

I have finally come to understand that my life is a perfect reflection of what I really want. I discovered that regardless of what I thought I wanted, deep down, in the place that really counts, I wanted to avoid ever having to face that emotional conflict again. That was my greatest desire; it's what I directed the power of my intention to create for me. I thought I wanted passion, to feel alive, and to love. Those turned out to be wishes; what I really wanted was to be free from the fear that feelings could bring.

Think for a moment of the patterns that keep recurring in your life. Perhaps you have regularly drawn the same kind of person in relationships, or have a recurring pattern in employment. Maybe you find that you push away anyone that gets too close, or constantly give to those who seem incapable of giving back. Maybe you think that you hate this and wish it would never happen again. All those events that keep popping up in your life have this in common. Your life is a perfect reflection of what you want most. No matter how much you say you want them to go away, in some deep place inside where you never go, they are a reflection of what you want most.

Intention is the force behind those patterns. Yet our own intentions can remain all but invisible to our conscious minds; it takes some effort and usually the help of friends who are better able to notice our patterns and can help us see them. Other people can often be more objective about our lives. If we can be open to their input, they can help clarify the patterns that have us stuck.

To understand how intention affects your life, think of it as a hidden program in your thinking. This program is constantly guiding your thoughts and actions to achieve a predetermined outcome. These outcomes are often contrary to what we believe we are trying to achieve. Though they may have served us at one time, they now have no "apparent" benefit to us and have clearly become liabilities to our success. Most people can't accept that this is going on inside them and that it is in their control.

Recently, I was working with a department manager who was having a problem at work. He was competent as a manager in every aspect of his job but one: he kept chronic underperformers on his staff. He'd try beyond reasonable means to fix their problems. When he couldn't fix them, he would take on the work they couldn't do. His boss was quite clear with him that this problem had to be addressed. He would agree with her in her office on a course of action that would have him confronting the problem person head-on. Unfortunately, when the time came to change his behavior, he would slip back into his routine of avoiding conflict.

What he didn't realize was that he had a hidden intention. He had decided early in his life that above all else, he would be a likable person. This was so deeply imbedded in his way of living that it operated automatically. When he made a decision to face his under-performer, he automatically did it in a way that allowed him to be liked. When he talked with his boss, he decided on an action plan that would have her like him. Unfortunately, there was no way that would allow him to discharge the responsibilities of his job and achieve his intention of being liked at the same time. His intention always won out, even though it was painful to his career goals and ultimately to his relationship with his boss and his self-respect.

His boss had suggested assertiveness training for him, but the problem couldn't be addressed by changing behaviors without first changing intentions. Each time the manager would try asserting himself, he felt like he was violating his values. Even though being more assertive made sense to him and was a reasonable request, he couldn't sustain the effort. His deepest intention always drove his behavior, regardless of what his rational mind said. He finally concluded that being nice to everybody was just the way he was and that to try to change it was futile.

This is a difficult process, but one that can be achieved by most—if they understand that the roots of their behavior lie in their intention. This is so difficult to truly get a grip on because it means that we are responsible for the outcome of our lives; the power to change is in our grasp.

That manager was never able to become free. He and those around him recognized what he needed to do differently to be more effective. He, unfortunately, never found it in himself to speak the unspoken truth in his life—the truth that he had decided that above all he would try to make the person he was with happy in the moment he was with them.

This is where the real power of intention becomes important to who you are today. If intention were always an unconscious force over which we had no control, then it would be of little use. The only purpose for knowing it would be to understand the past. Intention, though, is a power that is present and available to you today. Unfortunately, it is difficult to access and doesn't always work in the way you would hope. It is no genie in a bottle waiting to fulfill your wishes. It is a potent force that will allow you to alter the course and results in your life.

I began to understand it better only when I first told the truth about my patterns. You may remember that I said I had little access to my feelings at one point. When I began to work on why, I tracked the pattern back to an event in my childhood. This is where I encountered the first trap. I saw my life as having been a result of my parents' actions. I felt the pain of it and spoke to them about it. As a result, I felt emotionally better, but there was no real change in my behavior.

All I had really done was to play a game of emotional tag. I had been carrying a burden, and when I spoke to my parents, they now felt the burden I had handed off to them. I still had no real claim of responsibility. I have watched others get stuck in the same trap. There are many workshops, speakers, and books that encourage that behavior, and some people never escape. The result of their "growth" is that they are victims, and that's that. To understand intention first requires a statement of responsibility.

Upon genuinely claiming responsibility, an amazing process began for me. I had always seen my life as a linear path. It seemed like a movie to me. Each moment was like another frame of the film. Each frame was sequential and in order. I knew I was the way I was today because it was one step along the path from yesterday. I knew that tomorrow I would take another step on that path. Each new day was a continuation of the previous day and I was very much the same from one day to the next.

I remember having thoughts in school that I couldn't wait for the next semester because I would get to start over again. I remember making the same simple promise the first day in each new semester of school. I would sit with a brand new notebook that came to symbolize the fresh slate. I would tell myself that this year I would start off by doing all the assignments completely and on time and that I would fill that new binder only with class notes and homework properly done. Within a week, that book would be covered with the doodles of a daydreamer who wasn't paying attention, and I would already be behind in my class work and homework.

I remember that same feeling when I would move or begin a new relationship. There was always that hope that the slate would be washed clean and that I could start fresh. Sadly, I took myself on each move and new semester and into each new relationship and that clean slate always ended up the same as the old one.

When I started to see myself as responsible, I became aware of seeing myself like that roll of film. I noticed that I had been living as if the movie of my life began with my parents. It occurred to me that I saw them as archers and I was their arrow. They had picked a target of the right and proper life and let that arrow fly.

Like in a film, each day that arrow moved one frame. The next day it could only have moved one frame in distance and still pointed at that same target. Each day of my life, I saw myself as the same person—just slightly removed from the day before. There were times that I would struggle and resist but in hindsight, these times were really only window dressing. During the sixties when as a teenager I decided to exert my individuality, I bought bellbottoms and beads and dressed identically to six million other people exerting their individuality. All I had really done was change the clothes on the arrow. I was still moving as if my parents were the responsible ones and I had no real choices.

When I began to understanding intention, I realized that my life was the way I had wanted it to be. I hadn't been proud enough of who I was or believed in myself enough to want to be responsible, so I believed that it was my parents' doing. I was safe. I also began to understand that there was no freedom in a new semester or in being a new person in a new town. I now knew that in the next frame of film I could shift the direction. At first, I was hesitant to move it too far, but in time, I felt confident to follow my own heart.

Yesterday does not make me who I am today. I am not a victim to the path someone else set me on. I don't have to be a reflection of who I thought I was yesterday or an hour ago, or two seconds ago. I am not tied to my past nor is it directing me to my future. Strangely, when this became clear I realized that this is what my parents had hoped for all along.

The Unconscious Source of Intention

"Man's search for meaning is the primary motivation in his life."

Viktor Frankl

Finding meaning is important to us not only as a way to make our lives satisfying, but also as a way to make our suffering tolerable. This process is so important that we seek it in our conscious and unconscious minds. Many of us found in our earliest days a "meaning" to live for. These meanings are very different than the consciously chosen meanings that Frankl had in mind. This is a deeply ingrained decision to be a certain way regardless of the consequences. It's as if we formed an intention of how we wanted to feel about our "self," and how we wanted others to respond to us. As adults, this has become so automatic that we don't even recognize its presence, yet it is present with us each day, in nearly everything we do.

When seen in the clear light of understanding, it seems unbelievable and a bit simplistic. The manager I referred to previously couldn't accept at first that his life was guided by the hidden desire to be liked. It didn't seem reasonable that he would sacrifice so much for what seemed so little. Even when he was faced with the realization that the sum of his behaviors was best explained by his need to be liked, he had a difficult time with it. He also was startled by how difficult it was to consistently change his behavior.

Recognizing intention is difficult for a few reasons. I suspect that to understand who we are we need to know that we may have begun deciding what we would make of ourselves before we knew how to talk. From our earliest days, we may have been making decisions based on feelings, desires, and experience. We couldn't name them because we had no words. Imagine a baby's mind; he has wants, needs, desires, and feelings; he can think, but he hasn't yet learned any language. Try thinking for a moment without using any words; to most of us, this seems preposterous, yet it is all we could do for our first few years, and have continued to do so in our unconscious mind. To think, our minds are operating in feelings, pictures, and urges that don't always seem to make logical sense.

We have been making agreements in this way—about how we would live, what we wanted, and how we would go about it. This is accomplished in these natural forms of thought, not in neatly organized thoughts made of language. We began this when we were so young that we would have had a difficult time remembering it in any event.

As we aged, we became more and more conscious of what we think in the language in which we were raised, not in the language we were born with—pictures, feelings, and urges. Yet we have continued to make new decisions and reinforce our early ones in that same more primitive part of the brain. These decisions are some of the most powerful influences under our control regarding how our lives turn out. As important as they are, most people remain unaware of the existence of these decisions.

By law, it would be illegal for an agreement made at such a young age to be enforced. In fact, we enforce those agreements within ourselves, often in self-destructive ways. We have been taught to be clear, logical thinkers who freely use language to describe who we are and to express our thoughts. Many people mistakenly think that's *all* they are. They are only what they can consciously express or think about themselves.

Have you ever wondered why you have a hard time changing habits or actions? You can easily picture and name what you want to become, but find it almost impossible to become it. We commonly find ourselves in situations thinking we want things to go a certain way and not understanding why they always turn out differently.

I have a friend who says she wants to be in a committed and intimate relationship, yet she invariably chooses partners who are afraid of commitment and intimacy. When confronted with the concept of intention, she examines her thoughts and finds no hint of a deep intention. She only sees her conscious wishes. She concludes her intention is what she was thinking about.

There is an old story from Idries Shaw about looking where there is light. In the story, a man walking at night came upon another man searching on his hands and knees for a lost key under a streetlight. The two looked together for some time without luck when the second man asked the first if he was sure this is where he lost the key. The first man responded that he had actually lost it on the dark side street. When asked why he was looking here rather than there, he responded that the light was better here.

As silly as this story sounded when I first read it decades ago, I remembered it years later after meeting enough people who had been doing the same thing, looking where it is easy to see, instead of looking where the truth really lies. We consistently look where there is the most light, not in the important areas of shadows.

My friend can't make sense of this concept because she examines the parts of herself that are most convenient to see. She looks where the light of conscious thought falls—not in the shadowy depth of her self. She has been over it dozens of times and always concludes the same thing: "There must be something wrong with men, at least the ones I know." She can't see that there is an unbelievably powerful force at work shaping her destiny. What's even more exciting is that this force is the power of her own will, working to achieve her deepest intention. She, like the department manager, won't change until she taps into a deeper part of herself. It takes time and courage to explore the shadow within. It is easier to look where there is light, at the actions of others, or the circumstances of fate. These are easy to see, to blame, and to surrender responsibility to.

The concept of intention has been presented through books and the printed page for at least the last 30 years. I often see that people pick up the *language* of intention without truly understanding the message. I remember one woman who, upon hearing the idea, felt that she had gained a keen insight into her behavior. She was a divorced mother of teenage children. She was getting by financially, but it was a struggle. She had been blaming her struggle on her ex-husband who had left her and the children. She felt clear now that the divorce was somehow her intention, and as to the challenge of being a single mother, that was her intention too. In fact she had developed "20\20 hindsight intention." Each event in her life she now knew to be her intention. She didn't understand why or how—she just knew it was so. Had a bus run her over, she would have said that she intended it. If she was struck by a meteorite, I'm confident that she would have claimed that also had been her intention.

Her language had taken on the appearance of responsibility, but she was acting in the same fashion as always. She seemed to feel as if she were in control of a chaotic life just by claiming responsibility. It brought her comfort to believe she was in control. It never occurred to her that had she truly been in control, she never would have chosen the results she was getting.

She spent her time reciting the mantra of "That was my intention" as if it were some kind of magic spell. It was as if she were walking toward the future facing backward. She could clearly see all the things she had passed but nothing that was coming up. She was completely incapable of seeing how her actions were affecting her life but she "knew" they were. She took comfort and delight at noticing how her intention had created the situation she had just been through.

At the same time, she was creating new problems by bumping into the obstacles that could have been avoided had she turned and faced the present. This would have meant that she would have to be willing to not only comprehend the meaning of intention but also have the desire to change it.

I have come across a strange phenomenon in my work in personal development. Over the years, I have encountered a number of people who wander from seminar to seminar on a path of personal growth. They are always reading the latest book or attending the newest seminar in search of new insights. Oddly, some of them have powerful and unique insights into who they are and why they are the way they are, but it never seems to affect how they live. After each new experience, they are "lit up" about what they now know and then they immediately look for the next opportunity for learning. They act more like hobbyists whose hobby is collecting insights. After each new experience they share, the new insight with their friends just like a stamp collector would share his latest rare or unusual stamp. The stamp collector would no more imagine putting that stamp on an envelope for use than would an insight collector put their insight to use.

This woman was like a person driving backwards down the freeway collecting information on what was causing the wrecks she was passing along the way. She had insight about why her life was the way it was but refused to turn and see how it will be. The last time I talked with her, she had finally figured out why her marriage had fallen apart without noticing that her "new fiancée" was identical to her last husband.

The hope I have in writing this book is that it will be read and used not just to understand what happened, but to help look ahead. What is your intention? Have you decided to be "likable" as in the story of the manager, or to avoid feelings like I had? What is your underlying intention and what will tomorrow bring as a result? There are, as you will soon discover, a whole host of intentions from which to choose. When you become clear about yours, you will be able to begin to understand how it affects what you are doing now. You will see how it impacts not only your relationship but whom you choose for a relationship. You will notice how it affects your work and whether it enhances or impedes your career.

Then you will be able to use it as a tool that will help you to foresee and adjust your behavior to avoid falling into the pitfalls on your path. Until then, you will be like the woman walking backwards into your future. You will notice the mistakes you have made and may even feel responsible for them, but you won't see the mistakes you could avoid if you understood how your intention creates your patterns of behavior, regardless of what you consciously think you want.

Things to Remember:

1. **Many intentions were created without our realizing it.**

2. **Our conscious thoughts often contradict our deeper intention.**

3. **Our intention will overcome what we consciously think we want.**

4. **Intention is the most powerful force that shapes our characters and choices.**

5. **Intention is the cause of the long-standing patterns we experience.**

The Second Choice of Freedom

4

The Unspoken Truth

"Ye shall know the truth and the truth shall make you free."

John 8, *King James Bible*

There is an incredible liberation in truth. Left unsaid is that, until you know the truth, you live in a prison of ignorance even though you may be proclaiming your freedom. We live in the land of the free and have come to believe that freedom is our birthright. The truth is that freedom is our opportunity, not our condition. Unlike those people who live in a repressive political state, you may live in a repressive personal state. It is not an external tyrant that imprisons you but the tyranny of self-imposed ignorance.

When it comes to telling the truth, many people believe themselves to be honest, forthright people. What they often mean by that is they don't tell lies (except under dire circumstances or the occasional white lie). This is a far different thing than revealing the truth. I am not talking about the difference between truth and lies; I am talking about the difference in the quality of life that is only obtainable by revealing the unspoken truth.

This is the second choice of freedom. Will you choose to reveal who you truly are, or have you decided to remain masked and unknown?

If your honesty goes as far as not telling lies but stops short of revealing yourself, then you will stay forever hidden behind the mask of personality and will never find your way to freedom. Revealing the unspoken truth means you have to dig into parts of your life that have remained hidden behind a veil of unconsciousness. The task of becoming aware of what is hidden inside can be a daunting one at first. After all, how can you be expected to just *know* what you haven't known about yourself? Can you will yourself to become aware of your unconscious thoughts and feelings and how they affect your life? The answer for many of us is yes, as long as we are willing to explore our shadow.

Exploring Your Shadow

It has been over a hundred years since Freud introduced the idea of the unconscious mind. Even after all these years and volumes of work on the subject, the prevailing belief is that this "doesn't affect me." Most of the people I speak with may acknowledge the existence of an unconscious, but haven't explored the impact on how they live or who they are. The self-perception of most is that they are just who they think they are and that their motives and behaviors are clear to themselves and to others. "I am what I am" as Popeye says. This has come to mean, "I am as I believe myself to be."

In many lives, there is an important truth that is integral for finding freedom. Often this truth lies beneath the surface of consciousness and is barely concealed from those who need it most. Other times, the truth may be partially known but not revealed. This happens both to individuals and also collectively, as a truth known but remaining unspoken by a group. The second critical choice of freedom is to reveal the unspoken truth.

There are hundreds of truths inside each of us, many of which are irrelevant to our purpose here. This isn't an archeological quest to dredge up all the secrets of one's life, but a focused hunt on a few very important ones. You need to answer an important question: Who do you believe yourself to be—and how is that different from who you really are?

Think back to the diagram of personality, shadow, and essence. Personality is who we pretend to be. There is no freedom in pretence. Under the surface is who we fear we are, and our reluctance to explore those fears keeps us from ultimately finding freedom.

There are strengths and abilities hidden in your depth. There are aspects of your character that you have seen in others and wished for yourself, never realizing that you had them hidden in you all along. There are creative ideas and solutions to the issues that face you as well. In each of us there is an area of shadow. In the depth of that shadow, you possess knowledge about yourself that isn't readily available to your conscious mind. Because it is difficult to access and—occasionally embarrassing as well—you may have ignored how important it is to your success. That ignorance deprives you of your freedom. As counterintuitive as it sounds, you have hidden your strength as well as your supposed weakness behind a veil of unknowing. As much as you would appreciate and enjoy the strengths, you will be denied access until you are willing to reveal the whole truth.

To find out who you believe yourself to be, you first need to understand your intention. You have to truly come to grips with what you have secretly wanted that has made your life the way it is. Remember that you are not a victim. When you discover your intention, you need to know what you're currently doing to stay stuck. How is that intention playing out in your life? How is your intention keeping you imprisoned? When you uncover this, you will find the secret gifts that you are missing by hiding part of you.

To begin, think of your awareness in the simplest terms.

Studies on human consciousness seem to agree that you are unconscious of most of what goes on in your brain. The estimates I've seen indicate that you are conscious of about 3% to 10% of your mental activity. Most of what you don't know you don't want to know. Old irrelevant memories, mental processing mechanics, and some metabolic functions are better left unexplored.

Aside from the irrelevant details, there *is* some critical information in that 90-97% of unconscious material. The challenge of how to access it starts with understanding what divides the conscious and unconscious. When I ask that question in groups, the most common response I hear is "fear." Many people say they are afraid to discover what may be lurking inside. Fear may be a factor in *where* the dividing line is drawn, but the line isn't *made* of fear. Oddly enough, the geography of the brain is a little like a map of the United States. What's the dividing line made of between two states? It's an imaginary line that we create out of convenience. This is also true inside you.

The dividing line between your conscious and unconscious is an imaginary line placed as an act of convenience. Fear of what you may discover may influence where you place it, but ultimately you decide on its placement. You can move the dividing line to become more aware of your shadow simply by focusing on it. You can also get support from those who know you well and are willing to be objective.

Curiously, even though you may be unaware of the obstacles and limits you place on yourself, those who know you best are likely to be well aware of them. They have probably been trying to tell you about them for some time and are frustrated by how hard it is to get it across to you. Ultimately, you may wish to use the services of a trained professional. No matter how you start the process it is one that must happen if you want to use the full measure of the gifts and abilities you were born with.

I think my friend Kate is a good example. I have known her for the last 15 years. When I first got to know her, I noticed that she had a way of "sneaking up" on people. I first remembered her as someone who stayed on the outskirts of the group. She was always attentive but not terribly outspoken or assertive. She would, however, "sneak up" by having the most interesting comments and observations. She would find those opportunities when something important was left unsaid and no one seemed to be about to say it. Then without warning she would speak up with a comment or question that would hit the mark. She would then drop back into obscurity while the group came to grips with her comment; only offering more if the group misunderstood or didn't fully appreciate what she had said.

Kate always reminded me of a sniper in that you never saw her comments coming. She was nondescript in dress and manner. It was as if she was camouflaged and didn't want people to expect anything from her. Eventually, I learned that she had an exceptional scholastic career, was well read, and was quite articulate, but wouldn't show it if what she had to say was very different from the consensus of the group she was in.

As I watched her through the years, I wondered why she felt the need to disguise her talents. Why was it so important to sneak up? Initially my question puzzled her. She was in touch with the benefits and justifications and was proud of what she had accomplished through her style. She wasn't aware of the price and was a little resistant in examining it. Kate described what she came to call her "cloak of invisibility" like this:

Staying in the background seemed to work well for me in several arenas; as a girl in a "guy's world," I was never accused of being "too aggressive," or the (then) dreaded "b-word." As an academic over-achiever in a setting where brainy girls were generally outsiders, I learned to have a "good personality," and managed to stay included, at least on the fringes. In high school debate competitions, I learned how to make my partner look good, quickly finding and handing her statistics to use with her more authoritative voice, which meant she consistently outscored me. (But that was ok!)

I gradually became aware that it was useful to stay very quiet most of the time (which I was doing anyway) and occasionally say something very astute and on target, thus amazing everyone, which was often followed with being encouraged to speak more often. ("He who is last shall be first!") I relished comments like "You don't say much but boy when you DO....!" I found that I really enjoyed startling people with occasional brilliance, and adhered to Abe Lincoln's philosophy: "Better to remain silent and be thought a fool than to open your mouth and remove all doubt."

Despite her resistance, Kate started to realize that her behavior was in part based on the decisions she had made while growing up. As she examined her life in more detail, this is what she discovered about her unspoken truth.

I believe I have spent my whole life fine-tuning this now-habit of trying to remain invisible; anything that practiced does become a skill, and anything you become good at is hard to give up, even when it is no longer serving you.

....and it has served me well in many ways, at least in the past. Staying "below the radar" was practically a survival skill when I was very small. Our family was huge, and there was always a lot of extra work to do for whoever was "handy"; my father had a volatile temper and would sometimes kick whoever walked by him, and the sheer privacy I craved was very hard to come by, until I learned to "hide in plain sight"— up in a tree, in a corner of a closet, in the shadows of a shrubbery overhang, in the darkness between two outbuildings—all places where I could hear how urgently someone may be needing to find me, if necessary.

Learning to be very quiet and unobtrusive served me very well also in Catholic school, I found. The scary-looking all-black-clad "sisters," who seemed to be in charge of everything, including when and if I could use the bathroom, did not appreciate us speaking out of turn, and this was often dealt with severely. I have always been a "quick study," and it wasn't long before I was afraid to talk at all, and my voice became very small. When I was called upon to answer a question, it seemed I was forever being told to "speak up."

Besides all the behavioral reinforcement for becoming a silent non-entity, there was steady theological inspiration to explain the virtues of pursuing this as a way of life. In this very religious setting, we often read about the lives of the saints, who were invariably praised for their humility and their unassuming manner, no matter how great they were "inside." In addition, the daily New Testament readings in church would be parables or stories with themes such as "He who is last shall be first," "Blessed are the humble" and "It is easier for a camel to pass through the eye of a needle than for a rich man to enter the kingdom of heaven" (and this was the only goal worth pursuing, after all!)

Kate had discovered a part of her hidden intention, "to be invisible." It became apparent to her early in life that the best course of action for her was to go through life unnoticed. It was a wise decision for a child to make given the circumstances. Kate had also found a way to live with that decision. She was convinced that the reason she hid was that it was a noble and wise way to be. She still aspired to the characteristics of the saints she had so admired as a child. She thought of herself as being purely motivated by what was best for humanity. She believed that to call attention to herself was an act of self-serving egotism that lessened her value as a person. She also recognized the advantages she had developed through her disguise.

This way of living had become such a habit by the time I was an adult (in age, at least), that I was totally unaware of it. I was aware by then that not everyone acted in the same way, but I was just glad I didn't "need" to be the center of attention, and continued to work on perfecting my humility. By this time, however, I had also become aware of my need to make a difference in the world somehow and yet felt powerless to even touch that concept, since it seemed to require something outside how I operated – notoriety. So, I settled for doing what I could get done in the shadows, and began to recognize that I had learned a lot of very useful "people skills," such as how to get a group of people working together, how to "implant" my ideas into their heads (and be satisfied with NOT getting credit!), and especially, how to get someone else to step into the lead role.

Looking back now, I mulled over what it was about my "cloak of invisibility" that I had found so useful, so comforting, so hard to let go of completely, even now. Though I no longer have the time and immense energy it takes to maintain the illusion that I remain somehow unseen and unknown, there were (and are) still times that I prefer to think of myself as invisible, not publicly or openly committed to any one thing. It can be very satisfying still to come out of the shadows to surprise and amaze, rather than claim a spot "upfront" at the outset. (Claiming my spot would suggest that I have something worth hearing, which means I'd need to actually reveal that I had prepared, rather than make it appear as a spot of unexpected and casual genius!)

When it came time for her to examine her unspoken truth, she first had to understand that her "invisibility" was not motivated by humility as much as safety. This was no small undertaking. Kate was familiar and conscious of all the reasons that justified her behavior. She was adept at pointing out the many advantages of her style. She had already been dealing with the unresolved feelings of her youth. She had taken the risk to reveal her feelings but had continued to hold on to a self-limiting belief. She had been unable as a child to stand up to her father's raw emotional outbursts and achieve a just result. She also had been saddled with the expectations that she take on an adult's role as a child. As the oldest, she had felt it her responsibility to bring order to the house and to protect her brothers and sisters. She knew she couldn't achieve this through direct and straightforward communications because her father didn't respond to that. She had coped with this by learning invisibility, to quietly encourage frightened younger siblings, to (sometimes) "manage" her father by baking his favorite desserts, or infuriating him with her "go to hell" glare she could claim was out of her control; in short, she learned to control situations without appearing to be important, or to stand out deliberately. This was genius as a child, but she had never found a way to undo the assumption that she could only achieve her goals through such roundabout and indirect means.

Kate had to speak the unspoken truth about being "Invisible." That meant she would have to acknowledge the strength that had been dammed up inside and finally give it a voice. She had to let go of the idea that she was still a powerless child. As a child, she feared her father's anger and knew she wasn't big enough to stand up to him and express her needs without being beaten down. Like Lisa with the pack of wild dogs, she still viewed her fears and abilities with a child's eyes. She was still acting as if "they" were *all* big and she was still small and couldn't be effective. She had to take back her voice; she was still treating the world as if she was a helpless child who wasn't entitled to be heard. These were the unspoken truths of Kate's life.

I have to stress here the importance of first claiming responsibility for her intention. It was important that she recognize that she had *decided* to give up her voice and become invisible in response to her father. He didn't *make* her invisible; in fact, some of her siblings, raised with the same constraints, chose very different techniques to deal with his anger. (You will learn about Angie later.) The importance of this has been frequently brought home to me in the many times I have witnessed others (and myself!) finding those buried feelings and regaining our voices only to use them in the most irresponsible manner.

The Victim's Truth

The importance of making the choice of "I am not a victim" first and of accessing the unspoken truth next can be critical. If you remember the story I told earlier about my decision to avoid intense feeling, I became aware of the moment with my father when the decision was made before I became aware of my responsibility for making it.

As a result, I fell into what I call the victim's truth. When I shared what I had learned with my parents, the people I loved the most, it was from a point of view that they had caused the problems. I told them they had caused the suffering in my life and, as I walked away, I was feeling as if I had done the right thing and felt lighter. Sadly, it was more a game of emotional tag; I had tagged my parents with the blame for my failure. It was now their turn to carry the burden. Fortunately, we loved each other enough to work it out. What I had said was the truth *from my point of view at that time*, the point of view of a victim. Unfortunately, this wasn't a healthy one for me or for the relationship. Because I had yet to take responsibility for my intention, all I could share was blame.

A phrase that I hear regularly, one that makes me shudder each time I hear it, is "something *made* me do or be this way." I regularly hear it as an excuse for some supposed failing. It is said as if the person has no responsibility for how they are. I shudder because every time I hear it I know the person has surrendered their freedom. They aren't yet willing to tell the truth about their life. They have given up responsibility for what they did to create it and thus they have given up the ability to change it. They are stuck in the victim's truth.

As I had mentioned, although we may not be responsible for some of the events that occur, we are responsible for the conclusions that we draw from them. Let me explain with another example:

I was talking to a 35-year-old man who had never been in a committed relationship. He would either pick people who were relatively safe, people who were unwilling for some reason to commit, or, when someone got too close, he would start finding faults. He would then become distant and aloof until he managed to push the other person away. When I asked him why, he initially said he didn't know and that he was just waiting for the right person to come by. When he was questioned further, he admitted that one of his partners had in fact been the "right" person. and he had been so in love with her that it scared him.

Soon he was telling a story of his youth. He talked about his parents' divorce when he was nine. He told about how scared and lonely he had been when they split up. He also spoke about how he had thought that they had split because of him. The one truth he was finally able to admit was that deep inside he was afraid it would happen again. He feared that if he surrendered to love that he would somehow cause it to fail and his partner would leave him like his parents had.

As he told the story, a dam broke inside him. It was as though all the sadness from that terrible event had been held back until that moment when it came pouring out with the story. When he was done, he felt as if a great heaviness had been lifted from him and he felt he finally understood why he was afraid of commitment. He concluded it was because of his parents' divorce. He "knew" that his fear of commitment was their fault. At that moment, he felt healed and ready to continue his life. Sadly, he hadn't completed the process. He stopped, stuck in the middle of the victim's truth; he now believed that he couldn't be in a relationship because of his parents' divorce.

Cause and effect don't always happen the way we believe. We often miss our own contribution to the cause. Think back to a significant event that caused waves in your life like the divorce did in the man above's life. Now put that on hold for a minute.

Imagine for a moment that you are suspended above a large pool of water. Drop a pebble in and you can watch the ripples spread away from the center. Each ripple begets another until what was a still pool is now covered in waves. Each wave was "caused" by the one before; we tend to think this is true for us as well. Think of the pebble as an event in a life, like the one that occurred to you in response to the last paragraph. The first wave is a response to the event. The next wave is a response to the first wave, and so on with each additional wave.

When an important and unforeseen occurrence happens to us, we believe it works the same way. The event in the life of the uncommitted man was the divorce of his parents. He believed that had caused him to question his worth, which was the second wave. Because he questioned himself, he feared ever letting anyone close; this was the third wave. This caused him to keep people away, which made him pick people who were safe, and if they did become too close, he would push them away. It became "clear" to him that what caused him to push people away was the original event of his parents' divorce.

The flaw in this analogy is that we aren't exactly like the pool of water. The laws of physics that govern fluids and cause and effect are different than what happens in human consciousness. Think back to the original "splash" of his parents' divorce. Besides the emotional trauma that such a day creates, there is a subtle and often unconscious decision about the *meaning* of the event. It seems that we as people are always searching for meanings. It isn't so much the event that causes the reaction in our life but the meaning we place on it. After a little digging, he found the meaning he placed on their divorce was that he was somehow to blame, probably because deep down he was unlovable.

The event is difficult enough, but we have the ability to amplify or moderate the impact by the meaning we place on events. The pebble in his life caused the first splash, what *he thought* it meant caused the next wave and the ones after that. The man in question wanted to stop at the point where he figured out that his parents' divorce caused his fear of relationship. He benefited by dropping some of the leftover feelings of hurt and anger but never figured out the truth of how he interpreted their divorce. It was easier to blame them than to look a little deeper inside.

It turned out that when they separated he had started to wonder if it was his fault, that maybe he had misbehaved or not met their expectations. He made a secret promise to himself that he would do everything he could to save himself from that pain again.

Totally unaware of his own promise, he continued on with his life. As is normal, he felt the need for companionship and love, yet as soon as someone started getting too close, he would start to find fault with them. He convinced himself that he was backing off because of a problem *they* had. Ultimately, he would withdraw completely and begin the process all over again.

What he thought was that he just couldn't find the right person. The unspoken truth was that in the midst of his pain, he had made a promise to keep himself safe. His parents' divorce affected his childhood; his intention to be safe changed the rest of his life.

The decision that he was to blame for his parents' divorce was the real cause of the ripples in his life. When he finally spoke that truth, he was able to have a relationship without sabotaging it. His fear that he was unlovable was the first ripple. His intention to stay safe turned it into a wave. The way he stayed safe caused the next one, which meant never get too close. That begat finding fault with each partner he had. This led to criticizing to push the person away. Then the cycle would start over again.

As long as he thought his parents' divorce made him the way he was, all he could do was blame and mourn what "they" had done to him. Ultimately, he was responsible for his part in his life; until he accepted that, he couldn't move on. He had been stuck in the victim's truth, which always leads only to blame and self-pity.

Kate had at first found it easy to use her father's anger and the nun's strictness as the reasons for why she was the way she was. It was important that she claim her voice, not to use it against her father to set right the injustice of childhood, but to use it to claim her own freedom. As she examined her life more closely, she noticed that "invisibility" wasn't caused by her father or the nuns; it was a result of what she had come to believe about herself. Kate had come to believe that she was powerless to stand up to them as equals. "I can't get what I need or want through being straight-forward and direct" was the belief she was living out. "Knowing" that to be true, she resolved to turn invisible, only showing flashes of herself when it suited her needs. She had made herself that way in the face of her father's anger. Kate had found the decision she had made that caused her invisibility; she was past the trap of the victim's truth.

We aren't done with Kate and her quest for freedom. In fact, we are getting to the exciting part, the part where she resists the hardest. She had just discovered her intention, to be invisible. She still had to discover how that intention was playing out in her life, and what strengths were to be discovered hidden in her depth.

Kate had discovered part of the unspoken truth of her intention. But the most useful aspect of intention is what specific ways she was using invisibility. For Kate, as for many of us, invisibility was a string that confined her.

5

Strings

". . . for when I awaked it was just daylight. I attempted to rise, but was not able to stir; for as I lay on my back, I found my arms and legs were strongly fastened on each side to the ground."

Jonathan Swift, *Gulliver's Travels*

Gulliver was stuck. He wanted to move but found himself tied down. Kate had found herself in a spot that felt like that. She knew she wanted to change, to get up and get on with her life, but she was tied to a set of behaviors that kept her showing up as "invisible." When she had made the original agreement with herself (that it was best to be unseen) she, without realizing it, started to develop a set of rules of behavior. These are rules that she would have to follow to make her intention come true.

Rules for Living

Each person has his or her own set of rules. It's a code of behavior that you have to follow to achieve your intention. Think of your intention as a decision to always be a certain way. The rules for living are the guidelines to help us adhere to that way. For instance, when Kate chose to be an invisible person, one of the rules she had to live by was "Don't stand out from the crowd; always deflect compliments away from myself."

It has become a deeply embedded part of her character. She doesn't have to think about it; she just does it. It feels right to do it even when she recognizes that this is contrary to what she thinks she wants. Remember when she wrote: *"By this time, however, I had also become aware of my need to make a difference in the world somehow and yet felt powerless to even touch that concept, since it seemed to require something outside how I operated—notoriety."* Her rule of deflecting compliments was a string that kept her tied to invisibility. These rules are like the strings that tied Gulliver down. One rule by itself isn't strong enough. It takes several rules to tie you down. You may be able to recognize a dozen or more rules that tie you to a "way of being."

If, like me, you have more than one "way of being" then you're talking about a lot of rules. I used to wonder about what happened to feeling free; now I know. I had tied myself down.

Unlike Gulliver, who was tied down by Lilliputians, we have done this to ourselves. Others like mom or dad may have helped, but ultimately we did it. If you can't accept this, then you will stay tied down; if you think someone else got you stuck, then it will take someone else to free you.

As Kate became more aware of her invisibility, she noticed the secret set of rules she lived by. The rules are a logical formula to achieve the desired way she wanted to be. If you notice below, Kate's rules are all designed to help her arrive at the same place. If she had consciously designed them, she couldn't have done a better job.

Different people will pick slightly different rules even when they have the same end result in mind. We each customize our life to fit us just right.

Here is the list that she came up with when she delved into her rules to stay invisible.

Rules To Live By:

1. It doesn't matter if I get credit for success.
2. It shouldn't matter if I give credit for success.
3. My best is the least I expect of myself, and people should achieve without drawing attention to themselves.
4. We should be constrained in dress, appearance, and action.
5. Ambition is suspect; power should be shared in a group.
6. Don't stand out from the crowd, always deflect compliments away from ourselves.
7. Second fiddle can be an art form!
8. My best contribution is making other people look good.
9. I work most effectively behind the scenes; other people prefer (and are therefore better at) showmanship.
10. I shine best while hidden.
11. I am very good at quietly "greasing wheels."
12. "He who is last shall be first."
13. The best thing is to be humble; the worst would be thinking too highly of oneself.

Unfortunately, our rules often have a way of backfiring over time. The rules we live by often achieve our desired end result only in the moment. They are usually short-term strategies that will cause us more and more effort for fewer rewards. For instance, one rule of Kate's is "It shouldn't matter if I get credit for success."

This may work have worked fine for a while but not forever. Kate has taken on an enormous challenge. She has committed herself to achieve educational reforms in the criminal justice system, beginning at the local county jail. Having tried to push her ideas behind the scenes, she is finding one of the keys of leadership is to be noticed. In our society, we give allegiance to those leaders who have accumulated credit from their successes. The accumulation of credit also gives her the credibility to gain access to those people who can make a difference to the cause she supports. Kate knows this is true but doesn't like it. She thinks we should be listened to according to the merit of our ideas, that the ideas should get the credit and not the person. Philosophically I agree with her. In an ideal world, it would work just that way. Kate now had a tough choice to make. Was she going to wait for an ideal world before she made a difference in the jail, or would she change herself to be more effective in the world as it was?

Kate had decided to make the change in herself, albeit reluctantly. It just didn't seem right that she should have to change, and she was sure there was a way to achieve her ends and still stay true to what she saw as her "values." Over the course of the next few years, Kate was in a bind. She was struggling to come to grips with what her real values were and which of her behaviors were actually set instead only by rules supporting a youthful intention.

It was during this time that she became involved in our small support group. The group was formed to assist the members to stay on track with their goals and to give each other insights into obstacles that they may not see clearly in themselves.

Kate told the group she had come to a place in her life where she wanted to make a difference. She had recognized that that there are some changes she would like to see in the world. She had consistently tried to make those changes happen while staying hidden and working behind the scenes. She had been successful enough to feel encouraged but fallen short enough to know that something had to change. Even though she had fought it, she had begun to see that she might be the one that had to change if her dreams were to become realized.

As is common in a group like this, she started hearing that others saw her in a different way than she saw herself. She was starting to look in the mirror of other people's perception and saw a very different reflection of herself than she was used to (her own!).

She immediately knew that the group was somehow misinformed and she tried her best to share her truth with us. As a member of the group, I can say that it was by turns frustrating and amusing to watch the struggle.

The group was unanimous in their view of her as an extraordinarily powerful and committed woman who was still pretending that she wasn't big enough to stand up to authority and be heard. We believed she was still afraid of the "pack of wild dogs" and hadn't realized that they were actually Chihuahuas. She, on the other hand, believed that her desire to work behind the scenes was a noble and virtuous way to be, and based on her desire to do the best for humanity.

The disagreement wasn't over which was the right or wrong way to be; it was about who she really was. She had one view and was convinced that her view of the truth was accurate. The group saw that there was more to her than what she saw in herself. Together all of us took a stand for finding the unspoken truth.

Finding a small (ours had six) group of people who are insightful and objective can be a godsend for uncovering the truth about us. The key to our success was our willingness to take the risk of speaking truths that others were resistant to hearing, and doing so without judgment.

Oftentimes we have knowledge about other people that we keep to ourselves for reasons of our own. At times, this can be vitally important information that they need, and yet we have decided to withhold it. Likewise, they know things about us that we need to know. There is a socially accepted practice of withholding uncomfortable insights from each other. This is unfortunate in that others often have the best view of the parts we can't see in ourselves. Our friends and family can often be more objective and notice our long-term patterns without the interference of our justifications. If you can surround yourself with insightful people who are willing to share, and stay open to hearing what they say, you have given yourself the edge to gaining your freedom.

I remember one odd example from my own life that is so compelling because of the "story within the story":

I was lecturing to a group of about 40 people several years ago. At the time, I was talking about this very subject, trying to convince the group of the importance of getting good feedback. Knowing who you are without it is difficult, likely impossible. Most often, we see who we *believe* ourselves to be; finding the real truth can be facilitated by seeking the viewpoint of objective and insightful people. The problem is that many people won't share sensitive observations.

We were talking about the barriers that can constrain people in telling the truth. One that was especially troubling was the risk of hurting the other's feelings. It seemed to be true that one of the most common kinds of withheld information was that which might prove embarrassing to the hearer. This can be easily true even in a group of people who are actively seeking each other's input.

In an attempt to get those to reconsider their stand against revealing embarrassing truths, I made up a hypothetical situation. I asked them to suppose that I had by accident forgotten to zip up my zipper before I started speaking. Would they tell me the truth or would they refrain from bringing up a potentially embarrassing topic?

The group started to laugh and thought that this was quite funny. Upon further investigation, it turned out that I was either prophetic or unconsciously aware. (I had forgotten to zip up!) The group admitted that they had noticed this almost instantly. They further confirmed that, in fact, they had not told me to save me embarrassment. The irony is that they let me lecture for 30 minutes, each minute bringing more people into the conspiracy of silence, where *they* knew what *I* most needed to know. I was the only one in the room who needed the information. The sooner I knew it, the more I could save myself from looking like an idiot.

When I asked why they didn't speak up, they said it was to protect me; yet it was clear that their silence did me more harm than good. In fact, one woman, who I had assumed also had said nothing, had mentioned it, but to the woman in the next chair! She admitted that on second thought she wasn't protecting me from an embarrassing situation; it was herself that was being protected. She would have found it uncomfortable giving a vital piece of information to the only person who could use it. She was, however, easily able to share her knowledge with someone who *didn't* need it, actually contributing to the potential of the embarrassment she professed to be sparing me!

Sadly, the truth is often unknown because, at a deep and very personal level, it is more advantageous to be ignorant than informed.

Some of these truths are the unresolved feelings and self-limiting beliefs that I mentioned in the first chapter. If your self-esteem or self-respect is based on the idea that you don't have flaws, or at least that they are minimal, then this is likely the basis of your fear in knowing yourself. You may suspect that your self-esteem can't handle the knowledge. You could be one of the millions of people who believe that their value is based on their personality, instead of on their intrinsic value as a person.

The actual message we were trying to give to Kate was that her "invisibility" looked like an act; it "seemed" an aspect of her personality but we all felt we saw something far greater in her than she saw in herself. We believed that under her cloak of invisibility was a leader with an important message to be heard. Kate started to accept a new view of who she was. Then someone in the group had the audacity to suggest that they thought she wasn't acting as invisible as she thought; that somewhere inside she actually wanted attention.

That brought out a new level of resistance in Kate. She could initially accept that she might be hiding some of her power behind her false humility, but she had a much harder time accepting she actually might want and enjoy attention. At this point, she had one of those heaven-sent opportunities that arrived right on cue. It allowed her to see the unspoken truth in a new light.

I never even thought to question the merits of staying hidden, quiet, invisible, and relatively unseen. The only issue at hand was how to get my needs met anyway, though I'm sure I wasn't consciously aware of even that apparent (and inherent!) "conflict of interest." I hate to admit it, but in looking back, it appears I learned to use a lot of manipulative or passive-aggressive behaviors to get the attention I would sometimes need. This could take the form of hiding under the bed as a child longer than I needed to, waiting for someone to actually sound worried, of walking away from a party as a young adult, hoping someone would come find me, and even recently picking fights with the staff at the local Waffle House when they wouldn't allow me, as a solo diner, to sit at a booth instead of at the counter. There was apparently some part of me that was hurt and angry at not being "seen."

All was well enough, I thought, until one time when it wasn't—in a BIG way.

I was feeling particularly smug about my latest instance of pulling off another success while "disguising" most of my hard work. After working with a volunteer jail education program for several years (and studying criminal rehabilitation most of my adult life), I had managed to introduce a very successful and intense weekend into the jail setting. I was particularly proud of my slick (but hidden) manipulation of this very political setting; I had seized a perfect "moment" when a new sheriff was interested in looking good, and scheduled a meeting where several key players in the justice system (prosecutor, judge, parole officers) would be there to say good things about our past programs. This new seminar I was introducing was far outside the norm, and would require an unusual amount of trust and cooperation from the jail staff, but I managed to "low-key" it in that meeting, tossing it out on the table as "useful" (and only after we had been praised sufficiently.) "Oh, by the way, I have a new class we will be starting soon...." was how I slipped it in. The new sheriff, not knowing that my requirements for this class were unusual, and wanting to look cooperative, simply told me to set it up with his chief of police, who proceeded to walk me over to schedule it. I had already found a fellow facilitator whom I knew would leap at the chance to have some "floor time," even though he was a bit hesitant about doing so in a jail setting. I took care of that little problem the way I had always "manipulated" my other volunteer instructors into the jail over the history of our program; I asked him to show up at another class with another instructor, who "just needed another warm body in the room." (This low-requirement request would usually get people there and past their fear of the setting itself, once they were in the classroom as a "favor" to some other instructor.)

The seminar went off with nary a hitch, was more powerful than I had even hoped for, and quickly generated enough "buzz" that a local reporter asked to do a story on us. When he came to shoot some photos, I engineered the session so that my co-facilitator was in nearly every shot, while I remained behind the photographer, directing him, and making sure he had all his facts and spelling correct. I didn't even consider doing it any other way; this was habit by now.

The article was wonderful, generating even more excitement, and when friends and family would ask why I wasn't in the pictures, I just shrugged it off or grinned, explaining that I was directing the session just SO that I could stay out of the pictures. If I did feel a twinge of envy, I shrugged it off, congratulating myself again on "not needing" to be out front. By this time, I had a "support" group, who would tell me I needed to come out of the shadows, but I would counter that with calling myself a "master puppeteer" who knew how to "work" this highly political environment.

In fact, I was feeling a little smug about how much I had been able to pull off behind the scenes, and decided to take it to another level. There was to be a famous author in town whose new charitable foundation seemed to be in tune with what I was trying to accomplish. I decided to sign up for his seminar, with the intention of getting the article in front of him, knowing I had a better chance there, where there were only a few hundred people, than sending it by mail.

It all worked as scripted (in my head). I picked my moment, said something unusual and funny in front of the whole seminar (to get his attention), then on a break, I caught him in the hallway and gave him a copy of the article, telling him briefly about what we were doing. He seemed very interested; he even added that his foundation had been discussing prison programs, and promised to read it and get back to me. He also directed me to one of his staff, who took my information, and asked more questions. I also noticed I had become a "hit"; when I spoke, everyone listened; on breaks, several of his group would find their way to my table, asking more questions about the jail, and listening intently to what I said, even when it was explaining some point about what we were learning at the seminar. I was enjoying myself immensely, even gleeful about how I was pulling this off.

A few days later, I received a voice mail from a member of his staff, asking me to return the call. I couldn't resist telling a few people about it before I returned the call. In the meantime, I also received an email from his partner, asking how to get in touch with my co-facilitator (the one in the photos in the newspaper article.) I found this curious, but supplied the information. When I returned the call to his staffer, I was told that that they had received the info they needed (the contact info for the other facilitator) and "thank you very much." I was stunned, and I think I remember trying to remind them that I was the one who had brought them the article (or something equally weak) before I was dismissed.

As it turned out, they were interested in featuring "the guy in the pictures" on their website, as their featured "guest of the month." He was very flattered; I was very angry, though I was not sure at whom! This was, after all, my doing—my program, my idea, my mission, my work. This new "star" (my co-facilitator) was only a player in my play. He was a brilliant player, better than I could have hoped for, but he would have never been there had I not orchestrated the whole scenario! How could neither of them, neither the author that I had so admired, nor the co-facilitator who knew the whole story—see that? What was really jolting was the realization that this sudden "fame" was not in my control. The focus of the program I had worked so many years to establish, was now on the shoulders of someone I had recruited relatively recently, and who was not particularly attached to the jail setting. I was in danger now of watching my "cause" get the energy and attention to take off in a direction that would not serve it at all.

While I was feeling devastated, even betrayed, my support group (at least some of them) seemed to be delighted that I was facing such a great illustration of what they had been trying to tell me. I was so disappointed that it took me a few months to see the obvious; my role had not been singled out, had in fact been overlooked, because I had so successfully orchestrated it to be that way. I really had mastered invisibility, and it was not serving me now—at all.

That was a year ago. Since then Kate has continued her quest to find the unspoken truth. She has continued to notice the ways that she no longer can fit in the small box that her intention and her rules for living had created. Here is a recent story she told:

. . . so, I opened the newspaper last week and saw a column heading "Powers to Speak." Wondering what long-lost relative this might be, I read further, only to discover that the article was talking

about ME! My "humble" request to go to a local meeting to ask for jail volunteers had somehow turned into a "presentation" with "the public invited."

I had to chuckle; once again the contrast between reality and how I choose to see myself was smacking me in the face. My vision of sliding quietly into a meeting and meekly asking for a volunteer or two was out the window. What's more, in the days following the article's appearance, I heard from people who had seen the article and were planning to come, thereby guaranteeing that the group's numbers would swell that day beyond their usual attendance. "Oops, there goes invisibility—again!" kept singing itself in my head.

Like Kate, we have over time made assumptions about who we should be, as well as what we think others expect of us. In the end, each of us chooses a set of rules that we believe will suit us best. These are the ingredients that go into the mask that we wear each day. In time, the mask becomes what we truly believe ourselves to be. It also becomes the prison we're locked inside, just as Houdini was "locked" in.

We also have an expectation, even a need, for others to see us in the same way we choose to see ourselves. We fervently defend the image we have taken on. When others offer a different view, we assume that they just don't know us very well. If we want to know ourselves, we will have to find the unspoken truth beneath the mask.

Think how many times you have noticed traits or behaviors in others that they constantly deny. Just as you have had that experience with others, they have had it with you. Over the course of your life, people have been trying to show you pieces of yourself that don't fit into your image of yourself. While it may be true that some of those people may not see you clearly or may be off track, each of us knows someone whose opinion is objective and whom we can trust.

Sometimes the input is so consistent and from so many sources that it bears looking at. In my case, I had people telling me for years that they thought I came across as arrogant. In my view of myself, however, I was confident. I didn't want to undermine this strength by being swayed by the opinions of others. I also knew, as Kipling said, that it was important that I trust myself even when others doubted me; I thought that was another sign of confidence.

When I did think about this feedback, I realized that many people lacked confidence and were probably confusing mine with arrogance. I also suspected that other people might be jealous and were in fact trying to bring me down to their level. I decided to trust my own opinion and even tried to explain to those who were saying I was arrogant that it was really their problem, not mine. The more I defended myself, the more arrogant I *became*.

Finally, after a few years of this, I was open enough to listen and realized the truth in what they were saying. I was arrogant. Until I admitted that unspoken truth, I had no way to deal with it. It was affecting my personal and professional relationships. But because I didn't believe it, I couldn't see it. When I finally was open enough to listen, I found that the arrogance was part of a pattern; it was one of *my* rules for living that I played out each day.

Aesop wrote a story about the "Emperor's New Clothes." When I first read it, I assumed it was a silly tale invented to amuse us by the seemingly outlandish stupidity of the characters. Later I realized it was a teaching story designed to alert me to how people actually behave. The outlandish stupidity of the characters is quite common and, unfortunately, is as much about me as those around me. But I get ahead of myself.

You may recall that in the story, an emperor is taken in by a con man who convinces him that he is the best tailor in the world. The con man spins a tale of the incredible fabric that he is sewing into the most impressive and regal of garments. The emperor is so enamored by the story that he begins to "see" the garments when in fact the con man has taken his money and is sewing together a suit of imaginary clothes. The emperor has begun to see what he *believes* to be true instead of what is actually true.

As the Emperor tells his subjects of the upcoming clothing, the townspeople start to spread the tale, and it soon becomes known that the most incredible garments in the world will be adorning the king.

When the day arrives to show off his wonderful new clothes, the tailor helps him don the imaginary suit and the king walks out of his palace to the delight of his royal subjects. The emperor is, unfortunately, naked. The crowd, however, sees him as they expected, wearing the finest of raiments. They see what they believe to be true.

The emperor is pleased; the subjects are pleased; everyone is satisfied, with the exception of one small child who sees only the truth. The child is not deceived by the common understanding that the emperor is dressed in the finest of clothes and couldn't possibly be naked. "The emperor is naked!" he cries. The child has spoken the unspoken truth. His words reveal to the many what they could not see for themselves. It is as if a veil has suddenly been lifted from their eyes and they now see the emperor as he is, instead of how they expected him to be. Sometimes all it takes to change our perception of what is true is for one person to say what we were unable to say or unable to believe.

(On another day in a similar story, the child says the emperor is naked and everyone looks at him in shock and he is hustled off to bed without supper and severely reprimanded about inventing such lies about such an important person. He may even be sent in for therapy and medicated to stop the hallucinations!)

Sometimes the unspoken truth lies just beneath the surface and is ready to be heard; other times we just aren't ready to hear it yet. When this happens, we attack the messenger rather than hear the truth.

Our beliefs create our reality; what we believe to be true is what we act upon. The emperor believed he was buying the most beautiful clothes and that altered his perception of reality. He saw himself clothed when he was actually naked. When I first read this, I didn't think anyone could be so stupid. After having met enough people, I marvel at those who don't fall in this trap.

As for how the town people could be so easily fooled, "agreement creates reality." When in a group, people will often adhere to a group belief; the members of the group will come to agreement on what reality should be. The group members will then notice only those perceptions that concur with the common agreement. We see what we want to see. We ignore those truths that are inconvenient to see, that are incongruent with what we already "know" to be true.

What I find most interesting about this process is how pervasive it is. I had thought denial was a relatively uncommon problem, mostly occurring during times of great psychological stress. I find that in fact it is occurring for many of us much of the time when it comes to understanding ourselves. This was true of me and my arrogance. In a room full of people, I would try my best to convince them that my arrogance was in fact a beautiful suit of confidence.

Fortunately, there was always one person who saw the unspoken truth and was willing to risk telling it. To all of you who tried and whose words fell on my deaf ears, thank you. Even though I fought it to your face, after I heard it enough I finally woke up and saw the truth of it. By seeing the truth, I have been able to find more peace within myself, and to be less abrasive to others. This has been an immeasurably valuable part of my life's success.

Obviously, there was a lot of fear I had to overcome when I started to remove the mask and examine my self-image. I think another part of the problem stems from the fact that our eyes face outward, not inward. I can see others clearly; I can notice how they fit into their environment. It is apparent to me when they act congruously and when they make lame excuses to cover their own shortcomings. I also can notice their true gifts and the potential that they are blind to. It is easy for me to see the truth in others but to see myself I often need to borrow the viewpoint of those around me.

I was especially challenged because my arrogance prohibited me from admitting I needed anyone or that there was anything I couldn't do myself.

Perhaps the best way to reconnect with your personal intention is to examine long-time patterns. In looking at our lives, most of us notice ways that we have been consistent in certain kinds of situations. I have met people who let partners get only so close, then push them away, and others who completely give themselves away too quickly. Both find themselves in a series of broken relationships that look like the same relationship played over and over again. In time, they both feel stuck in a pattern of behavior that is frustrating, and from which there seems to be no escape.

What are *your* habits or routines that have repeated themselves over and over? Notice especially the ones that have been consistently aggravating. Where do you feel stuck? What are the areas of your life that seem to play themselves out time and again?

Kate also told me about Angie, her sister. You will see that, even though she was raised in the same family with the same circumstances, she decided on an entirely different way to live than her sister. Angie was a middle child of thirteen siblings who didn't get the attention she wanted. As an adult, she excelled in her work (an RN in cardiac care) and in some areas of her personal life, but she still never felt she got the credit she deserved. She always felt like she had to scrape and fight for both her own place in the world and for that of her loved ones. Because she could be, and often was, a fierce protector of her family and patients, people often viewed her as "angry" or with a "huge chip on her shoulder." Because she assumed it was necessary, Angie carried "readiness to fight" with her everywhere, so road rage and rudeness to clerks and wait staff were routine parts of her day. She didn't see this as unusual, since it had been a necessary survival strategy while growing up, and she had no reason to think the world had changed in her favor.

Angie hadn't noticed the larger pattern of her life. She couldn't see the connection that linked her behaviors together. To her sister, who could now stand at a distance and be more objective, it became easy to see only after working to understand her own intention. "Angie has been an enigma to all of us most of her adult life. (Why *does* she do these things? How *can* she be so obliviously dishonest? Don't expect *her* to show up where she says she will be.)" Angie had set her life up with a clearly identifiable pattern of rules to live by. Unfortunately for the rest of the family, some were significantly different than the rules they lived by. Unfortunately for Angie, she was often on autopilot with her behavior. Her list of rules looked something like this:

Rules To Live By:

1. You gotta look out for number 1—and your family—because no one else will.
2. If I let them know they can't mess with me at the outset, I'm more likely to win in the end.
3. No one hands you a break—you gotta scrape for everything you get.
4. I'll let'em see my anger, but I'll cry in private (if I have to cry at all).
5. Since people aren't going to accept me as I am, it is not always necessary—or even wise—to always tell them the truth.
6. The opposite sex is not to be trusted; they are too gamey. You can sometimes get what you need through manipulation, though.
7. If a commitment I made is no longer convenient or useful to me, it is ok for me to break it; they'd probably do the same thing anyway.
8. I work SO hard to get my family what they need; I can't believe how unappreciative they act toward me sometimes.
9. Life's a bitch, and then you die.

Angie had a basic underlying message to the world, "I must look out for myself." Without realizing it, this had become the thing she intended to do in every situation of her life. She looked out for herself and her family while driving, eating, working, or relating with others. She was so adept at it that, without any thought in any situation, she would protect herself and her interests, often with general disregard for others who were not within her "circle of protection." After all, they would be looking out for themselves as well. She had come by this philosophy honestly and in many instances, it had served her well. It had also cost her a tremendous price.

Angie had come to a point where she thought it would be nice to change, but she didn't know how to start. She could think of how she would like things to be, but she felt immobilized. Like Gulliver in Lilliput, she felt tied down, unable to move. She kept looking for the reasons that she might be holding back, but to no avail. What she couldn't see was that she was being restrained by many small ties like the thousands of threads that held down Gulliver. Each of the rules she had created was designed to help her "look out for herself." They had been tested over and over—and they worked, but at the cost of keeping her tied down.

Angie was immobilized, held back by the very rules of behavior that helped her look out for herself. The first step to freedom for her was becoming aware. She had to see that the underlying foundation of her struggle was in a set of agreements that she had made without knowing it. With her sister's help, she began to see the connection between her underlying intention and the way her life was working. The awareness itself started to loosen the bonds that were holding her back.

Her sister Kate said: *"This process of describing "ways of being" has actually changed our relationship. Instead of getting irritated with her (and periodically keeping my distance or blowing her off), I can see it now as part of a bigger pattern that she is rather helpless in seeing. We now have interesting and funny conversations about things we avoided talking about before. She calls me to meet and talk a lot more, and I no longer have to make the choice to be either an all-supportive co-conspirator, or a confronting older sister. Now we can just talk and laugh."*

Kate had uncovered the second choice of freedom and had spoken the truth about her life. Angie could not see this in herself and so is still tied to behaviors and a life that is frustrating. Her sister, however, was able to change her own feelings in the relationship through acceptance.

In the next chapter, I have collected a list of different intentions or "ways of being" that people have volunteered. I have also included their "rules for living" and some of the strengths and frailties that came with them. You may find yourself in those pages or you may find yours to be different. Take the time to write down what you suspect your rule are and take the time to "reality check" it with someone you trust.

Things to Remember

1. **The results of long-term patterns are the easiest way to notice your intention.**

2. **We have a consistent set of rules that supports us in our intention. Other people notice and try and tell us what they see in us, but we usually justify our actions to keep us from changing.**

6

Ways of Being

"If your only tool is a hammer then every problem looks like a nail."
Carl Rogers

Like Angie, people have unconsciously picked a way they would always be. Angie employs the same behavior regardless of the circumstances. On some occasions, this is appropriate and may be the best way to get her needs met. Other times, she comes across as untrusting, even angry or rude, ready to argue without any real provocation.

Angie's tool is to look out for herself; that's her hammer. Other people usually look like a threat to her, and many of them feel the effect of her blows. Over the course of her life, she had decided that, in order to get the most out of life. she must act or appear a certain way.

These "ways of being" are formed by the power of our intention and define the way we will act. They operate without conscious thought and often create results that are contrary to what we *think* we want. It's as if we have a silent guard monitoring what we say and do. This acts as a filter making sure that no "inappropriate" words or deeds escape into our lives.

Over time, a list of rules develops that become the boundary to how we can live. Even when the boundaries begin to feel more like a prison, we hold to the rules rather than change them. Often we know what we think we "should do" but find ourselves unable to do it. Sometimes, within moments of declaring that "this time, I will act differently," we find ourselves doing the same thing we always do.

People may think that their seeming inability to change is because they are weak-willed. I find the opposite to be true. I see them as incredibly strong-willed and tenacious. They just don't realize that the strength of their will is being used to hold onto a "way of being." You may have wondered, "What's wrong with me? Why don't I have the strength to change?" There is nothing wrong with you. You have tremendous strength, which you demonstrate daily by holding on to your intention. People think of children as being unreliable, but a child who acts with such clarity and conviction can make a promise that will last a lifetime. You have done a tremendous job of keeping your promise.

It is important to note that these "ways of being" are also the source of much strength. The behaviors that go with them may be most appropriate in some situations. In fact, much of what we admire about ourselves comes out through these behaviors. What makes them troublesome is the automatic way we use them in inappropriate situations.

You may recognize some of yourself in Nancy. She and those around her admired her for the tenderness, compassion, and concern for others. She has a genuine regard for the well-being of her family and friends. These are wonderful traits that she desires to keep. She would, however, like to regain control and act more consciously, especially regarding her own well-being.

Nancy had decided at an early age that she would always be "likable." That intention has led her to rely on and develop those parts of her that bring such joy to her and to those around her.

There are times, however, that she gives not from a desire to serve but from a compulsion to please. Often she finds herself giving too much of her time and energy to others, or not standing up for herself when people take advantage of her desire to please. Some of the prices that she pays could be lessened if she would say "no" more often. This will only happen when she learns to take herself off autopilot. The biggest problem with a "way of being" is that it operates outside of our conscious control. It's important to not throw the baby out with the bathwater, as you will notice the source of your greatest strength will also be found there.

Even though we all have our unique twists, there are some common "ways of being" that fit a great many of us. Although the following short list won't fit everyone, I have included it as an aid to help you in identifying your rules. As you read the list, notice your reactions. Sometimes, you will see yourself immediately and the definition will seem to fit you perfectly, or nearly so. Make a note of the one that fits best and reflect on how it shows up in your life. You may want to journal on how it affects your life, your relationships, and your feelings about yourself.

Many people will see themselves in more than one "way of being." If this is true for you, notice which one seems to be prevalent and which seem to be secondary. Think about how they interact in situations in your life. Make a list of the specific prices you pay for going on autopilot with those behaviors. Also, make a list of the rewards.

If you really want to challenge yourself, and to make it even more interesting, enlist the aid of someone who knows you well to assist in identifying the prices and rewards. They are quite likely to see a side to this that has been outside your grasp.

If another person has been affected by your behavior, you may also find that the resulting discussion would start to open up and resolve areas of conflict between the two of you. For this purpose, the person you choose should be as close as possible while still being able to maintain an objective view.

As you read them, notice which seems most familiar to you. You may recognize it by its intention or by the rules to live by. Don't be distracted by looking for the perfect fit. You may have to customize it.

You may find that your friends or family can give you keen insights into your style. These insights may be uncomfortable at first. The initial reaction is often "that's *not* me!" This is often an indicator of a good fit, as we saw with Kate

I Want to Be Liked

Nancy is liked by many people. Wanting to be liked is a trait she has had since childhood. She learned very young that being the clown and getting a laugh helped to make people like her. Her parents were well-liked, so they were able to teach her many of the rules for being liked. While she enjoys the positive attention she receives, she sometimes feels used and taken for granted.

Because it is so important for her to be liked, she has a tough time setting boundaries, and feels people sometimes step on her. It is hard for her to get her needs met because she doesn't want to ask.

She seldom argues because it may upset someone. She hopes people will like her simply because she is not threatening, and agrees to almost anything.

While she has many acquaintances, she has very few close friends because she is afraid to risk being authentic and letting her real feelings show. She obeys all of the rules even when she does not agree with them or they do not serve her. She winds up feeling that no one respects her.

Rules to Live By:
1. Don't make waves.
2. Keep opinions to yourself.

3. Never get angry.
4. Be funny—be the clown.
5. Appear pleasant at all times.
6. Give more than I want to.
7. Smile—even when it hurts.
8. Don't say "no."
9. Check other people's responses before having one.
10. Sugarcoat everything.
11. Avoid difficult communication; it may go away.

The strengths I have gained from these rules are: I have a way about me that is non-threatening and very open. Most people find me easy to be with and are comfortable talking to me about almost anything. I am compassionate, patient and truly care about others. I have a great sense of humor and add lightness, energy, and excitement to a room. Because of my desire to appear pleasant at all times, I usually find myself truly in a good mood, which has me smiling a lot. I am a good listener and have a desire to hear about the other person. I also have a keen insight and can 'read' most people pretty well. I am trustworthy.

It is important for me to be this way because I enjoy being around people and working with them on a personal level. When people (even strangers) approach me smiling and wanting to talk, I feel a sense of fulfillment. Seeing others laugh or just feel a little more special or better because of something I have said or done brings joy to my heart.

The price I have paid for this way of being is often when I am trying to please others, I am not being true to myself. Many times, I have sacrificed my own wants, needs, and desires. I have sacrificed responsibilities professionally, as well as with family, for fear of displeasing someone, especially anyone I view as an authority figure.

Because I am easy-going, I sometimes have trouble getting anyone to take me seriously. This presents a real problem when I am working in any leadership position. I also find myself stretched to the limit because I have such a tough time saying "no."

Ego Is Bad

Kate had a modest and unassuming demeanor. She cared deeply about the success of what she believed in. It was her way to give credit to others and stay in the shadows. She often was underestimated in that people were unaware of her contributions, her creativity, and her intelligence. Mostly she didn't mind unless she felt that those who received the credit used it to their personal advantage. She hoped that people would see through her modesty and realize her true value.

At home, Kate would spend what time she had left trying to catch up on housework or other unfinished business, while chiding herself for not getting more done towards her worthy causes. She felt guilty when she slept late, since there was so much still to be accomplished in life. She was also somewhat frustrated and bitter about her lack of career advancement. It seemed that people with more flash and less experience were passing her by. Here too, she decided that the truth would be known soon enough and that she would bide her time until she was recognized for her abilities.

Rules To Live By:
1. It doesn't matter if I get credit for success.
2. It shouldn't matter if I give credit for success.
3. My best is the least I expect of myself and people should achieve without drawing attention to them.
4. We should be constrained in dress, appearance, and action.
5. Ambition is suspect; power should be shared in a group.
6. Don't stand out from the crowd, always deflect compliments away from yourself.
7. Second fiddle can be an art form.
8. My best contribution is making other people look good.
9. I work most effectively behind the scenes; other people prefer (and are therefore better at) showmanship.
10. I shine best while hidden.

11. I am very good at quietly "greasing wheels."
12. "He who is last shall be first."
13. The best thing is to be humble; the worst would be thinking too highly of oneself.

I learned early to stay hidden. With ten siblings, there was always undone housework to be assigned to the nearest warm body. There was an exhausted, overworked father with a bad temper, who would sometimes kick the first person crossing his path. There was always chaos, noise, and accidents to clean up—or to be blamed for and punished.

I sought refuge in the quiet of church, where my early learning was reinforced and "explained" in the form of gospel lessons exhorting such truisms such as "He who is last shall be first, and stories of how the proud were brought low, how the humble would inherit the earth, and about how it was easier for a camel to pass through the eye of a needle than for a rich man to enter heaven, etc. Most of the saints I read about were poor, and the word "conceited" was the worst of insults, it seemed. I remember once while still very small, and being told for the umpteenth time that I was a "pretty little girl, I innocently replied, "I know" and was immediately deflated by my mother's horrified reaction. It was then that I learned not to pay attention to praise, and certainly never take it to heart. I decided very early to live a life seeking humility, and to stay out of the limelight.

This intention worked well for years. At school, in which I did well by quietly studying while others had "fun," I quickly learned that to be recognized for effort and achievement had a definite downside; though the teachers appreciated it, the other kids would sometimes call me "Brain," and in those moments at least, tend to treat me as if I were different from them somehow. Boys tended to shy away from the usual early awkward attempts at pairing up, though the brighter ones liked to talk to me.

One day, especially, sticks out in memory. The class had taken on a challenge from the Weekly Reader to learn to spell a 45-letter word (for a throat disease). Since it was a class project, several people achieved this, so it was "safe" to do so also. Until, that is, my older brother was dragged into my classroom by the ear, and made to stand and listen while his little sister spelled a word he could not even pronounce, as his class got the same newsletter a week late. He had been "set up" to be reading this particular article aloud at the time. I had no choice but to spell on command, and watch while the class laughed at my brother, a well-known and constant source of trouble with the nuns for his creative antics

So, I learned to hide my work, opting to study late at night after everyone went to bed (since that older brother was in the next grade up and could carry stories to the group). I also learned to play down any accomplishment, learning to be "bored" when my name would be announced over the high school speakers about winning a math competition, a debate, a national Latin test award—whatever. With all the religious guilt and learned humility I had taken on over the years, I knew it was all not really my doing anyway, that I just "knew how to take tests," had "figured a way around the math problem," and was "just lucky." Even photography awards were written off to good subjects, good models, good printers, or "luck." There was always a "reason" to discount any achievement. (Even now, I feel uncomfortable claiming these accomplishments; maybe I'll use a fake name here, the name's not important anyway!)

I did gain many strengths and skills as a result of this choice, particularly in the area of teamwork. Thwarted in "shining" creatively myself, I adapted by learning how to make the group shine as a whole. I learned how to implant ideas into others in a way that had them thinking it was their own, delighting in hearing someone make a point to me that I had given to them, though they did not remember the origin. In this way, I managed to get a lot of good done, and in a way consistent with my beliefs and values.

I felt very much a "master puppeteer," as I quietly mingled

behind the scenes to get people to do extraordinary things. T
a saying that wonderful things are achieved when no one ı ___ɔ
credit, and I found this to be delightfully true. Additionally, since I
did move in such an invisible fashion, I was also a non-threat to
existing systems that can be very resistant to change, and to egos
that don't like to be shown up by newcomers.

The price I paid was that in doing this automatically, even when
it may have been better to shine, I missed opportunities to make
even bigger differences. I instinctively avoided publicity, even when
it would be good for my causes. Without thinking about it
consciously, I viewed all such attention as misplaced, and would
only reluctantly be in the spotlight if someone could convince me it
would serve only to further the work.

I also deliberately shoved other people out in front, and stayed
in the shadows, which, for me, could actually be the lazy way out. It
also served to keep me exhausted (since no one knew all I was up to,
I was called upon for many such roles) and somewhat non-
committed; since I wasn't often publicly identifiable with any one
cause, I could easily drop out and go on to another.

It also dawned on me not long ago that I am still hiding my
work by doing the bulk of it in the wee hours of the morning; when
people are around, I go on autopilot to look like I'm not that busy,
regardless of how much I have piled up. It's really only when
everyone is gone that I can settle down to get serious work done,
and I think a large part of that is that old habit of wanting to not
appear like I'm exerting more than the usual effort. The downside is
that some people must wonder if I ever work hard, when in fact, I
rarely am not working—on something, for someone!"

I Must Protect My Position

Karen was given responsibility early in her career and quickly
was promoted to run a remote operation. She relished her
independence and resisted interference from the corporate office,

even from her manager who was a great mentor. Her manager wondered why Karen was suddenly being aloof and defiant, but didn't understand that Karen did not want to show weakness. Karen decided to take the risk to completely open up to her manager about her vision and her shortcomings. When she did so, the relationship became immediately strong, and led to another promotion to a larger group.

Rules to Live By
1. Ask questions.
2. A good offense is the best defense.
3. Sometimes I feel scared and don't want to admit it.
4. I am afraid of losing.
5. I'm the leader—I'm responsible.
6. Failure is a reflection of me.
7. People can take advantage if you show them your vulnerable side.
8. Bully or guilt to get what you want.
9. People won't respect you if you fail.
10. You can alienate yourself.

Protection seems like it should be very natural. Animals protect their young and armies protect their lines. So what's so wrong with trying to protect your position? At first glance, I thought I wasn't just protecting my position but protecting my responsibilities. Defending my ground (my employees, the operation, the culture), but after some thought, those were second to the defense. It was my ability to be effective that I was protecting. If I showed any vulnerability, it could be perceived as failure and failure is not acceptable. No one accepts defeat!!!

I always thought that by asking questions you were gaining better understanding. That's only the case if you take the time to listen to the answer.

The costs and the price you pay in losing shouldn't be the

reason for fear. Those that want to win, win for the right reasons. I am trying to win so I won't fail.

I Will Be Wealthy

Dan knew from an early age that he would be wealthy. He had developed an intuitive knowledge of how to make money. Convinced that this would make him happy, he constantly increased his wealth to counteract any unhappiness he felt. He became a well-known figure in the community, although some people didn't trust his motives. There was a perception that money was most important to him. Those who knew him best knew more about what he accomplished than who he was. They also had the feeling that the relationship was second to "the deal."

People often felt he was distant or aloof. Dan was usually sizing people up as to whether they could help him profit or not. The art of the deal had become the most important part of life and as a result, his marriage suffered from it.

Rules To Live By:

1. Everyone I meet has an opportunity in them.
2. Most people see the problems not the value in the opportunity.
3. I don't think about obstacles until I encounter them later.
4. I rarely think about prices until I have to pay them.
5. I immediately assess people's ability and will to participate in the deal.
6. I trust my own instincts more than anyone else's analysis.
7. I trust myself enough to bet the farm on a deal.
8. I sometimes bet the farm to keep myself fully committed.
9. I hire good role players but not competitors for what I do best.

By the time I was 12 years old, I knew what I would be when I grew up. Whenever anyone would ask I would answer I didn't know what I would do, but I would be a millionaire. Back in the 50s, this was a considerable amount of money, and I knew to my core that I would have it. From that point forward, the accumulation of wealth drove my life. The drive to be wealthy led me to an understanding that would make it possible.

Most people I've talked to have it backwards. They think that the knowledge of how to accumulate wealth comes first, that you discover the keys to success and then you realize your dream. I always knew my dream would come true and from that knowing came an understanding of what I needed to do.

Years later, after I had lived out my dream and created the wealth I desired, I began to look for the roots of my desire. After a great deal of soul searching, I believed I had found the core, the beginnings of my desire. At 12, the desire was already well set and seems to have come from an early age, around five to nine years old.

My parents used to fight with each other and the subject was always money. Through years of fighting, I started to believe that if you wanted to be happy in a relationship you need enough money. If you have enough money, there is no need to fight. I figured if I had enough money I would be happy.

I committed myself to be wealthy by 12 and I knew it without a doubt. I am completely clear that from that intention came the knowledge of how to have wealth. I just understood how to do it. They didn't teach it in school, and no one in my family had ever owned or run a business.

Other People Are More Important

All who knew her thought Adrienne was a truly considerate person. She seemed to exemplify the virtues of humility and self-sacrifice. She was a conscientious employee who handled not only the tasks of her job but also had the ability to handle stressful situations and stay on an even keel. Adrianne was as an indispensable employee and people often felt at a loss when she was away.

Adrianne brought those same qualities into her personal

relationships and, although they seemed to work in the beginning, her relationships usually ended in failure. She thought at times that maybe she was just bad at picking a partner.

Rules To Live By:

1. My needs are a burden and meeting my own needs does not create return justifiable enough to do so.
2. Everyone should show love the same way I do.
3. Be less important than everyone else.
4. Be indispensable by reading minds and anticipating desires.
5. Control people and situations by doing for them.
6. Let others' weaknesses become my definition of who they are.
7. Don't ask for help or show vulnerability.
8. Avoid social situations where I am not in a role of doing, helping, or otherwise contributing.
9. Choose friends and partners who do not/cannot meet their own needs.
10. Focus on the needs of others to avoid dealing with my own.
11. Dependency=Love.

My way of being is to put the needs of others before my own. There are threads of needing to be in control and feeling unworthy woven through my way of being, but the strongest drive for me is in needing to be needed, and subsequently expecting others to do for me as I've done for them.

The positive aspects of this way of being are valuable to me in my work as a special education administrator. I'm very good at "reading" people and sensing the emotional "temperature" of a tense meeting or conflict. I am an active participant in programs with my children-snack mom, room mother, PTO office, etc. Balls very rarely are dropped when I am around, and I can multi-task with the best of them. I am response-able. I can put my own concerns aside in a crisis and focus on the things that need doing. I can also easily switch between "wide angle" and "telephoto," meaning that I'm good at seeing both the big picture and the small details simultaneously, and can perceive interactions and relationships in both views.

The less advantageous aspects of this way of being show up in my personal life. I'm so focused on the emotions of others that I am very out of touch with my own, and I can be very reactive in this way. Anger is a sign I am not recognizing my own feelings. I feel disconnected and that I don't belong unless I have something to do. I tend to under-train my employees and children so that they will need me and my relationship with them can be supported by doing what they aren't able to do for themselves. When the kids are in bed, the housework is done, and there's nothing I need to do for work, I often sit immobilized and fearful. Anxiety is a constant presence in my life. I don't have many close friends because I can't do for them in the same way I can do at work and home.

The most significant impact that my way of being has had in my life is in my marriages. At 33, I've been married twice, divorced once, and am presently separated from my second husband. I choose men who have a demonstrated inability to meet their own needs, first emotionally, and in my second marriage, I have chosen a man who is presently unable to support himself financially. I chose to marry him because his neediness and dependence felt safe to me: he couldn't leave me because he couldn't make it on his own. His power-less circumstances made him appear to me to be less likely to leave me or stand up to my anger and martyrdom. Ironically, as I took care of him, I lessened the likelihood that he could give to me emotionally because he became more powerless and resentful, and ultimately left anyway. This is exactly how I had set the marriage up in an unstated dependency=love agreement—you let me take care of you and love me in return.

I Am Self-Sufficient

Elle was known as a diligent and self motivated business woman. Many who knew her thought of her as aloof and distant; they thought that was part of her professional demeanor. Those that tried to befriend her also found it difficult to get very close. They were only allowed to see the surface but never truly knew her heart.

Rules to Live By
1. Never let myself be scrutinized by anyone.
2. Never let anyone in.
3. I can manage my life by myself; I don't need any help.
4. I depend upon myself.
5. Don't expose any vulnerability.
6. Be an observer.
7. Create my own interior world where I can bury feelings.

I remember vividly making this secret promise to myself as I rode in the elevator at the Chicago Children's Hospital somewhere between the x-ray floor and the orthopedic clinic. We had just been told that I had severe scoliosis, which would require surgery. My then 11-year-old brain couldn't understand the impact this would have on my life, but judging my parents' reaction, I concluded it would be big. "No, no surgery," concluded my parents. They decided we would attempt to stop the curvature of my spine from worsening by wearing a brace from hip to chin.

I wore this brace for six years of my life. I felt defective, out of place, different. Just as I began to wear this brace, my family moved (yet again) to Cincinnati. As I went through my teenage years, I felt as though I had sunken into myself and my rules started to take effect.

As a child, it's simple and clear to claim this single experience as the one event that triggered my decision to be self-sufficient. As an adult, I can see that many things led to this decision; perhaps it was our family's moving every three years, or perhaps it was the emotional disconnect that frequently occurred between my mother and myself. Regardless, I entered into this pact with myself.

As time passed, I found myself becoming very selective of my "friends"—those whom I would allow to be friends with me—until it required some emotional investment and work, and then I casually would cease to be interested in the relation. I decided that sex was a form of intimacy and I refused to share that with anyone until I decided it was time. I felt as though everyone and everything was transient. It was important not to get too attached to anyone or anything.

My rules took over my life, and as I reflect now, I realize the rules I lived by created a life that did yield some tangible benefits. I am incredibly self-sufficient in my work. I work for myself and have established a business that most would have said couldn't work. I am my own boss, I set my own schedule. I can support myself and my daughter without anyone's direct help. I am very organized and efficient. I think of myself as being very adaptable. I value non-material things and take notice of beauty in the oddest of places. These are some of the rewards. Having worn a brace, I was able to learn early the ability to see beyond someone's physical appearance.

The cost? Complete isolation. It is only now that I can see the cumulative effect these rules have had on my life. I am just now learning how to understand my feelings and respect them and express them. I only now understand how to be a friend—a true friend, to myself and to a few others. This is such a gift. I had no idea how joyous this feels. I married a man with whom I had no intimate connection, a man who was as numb as I was. We are since divorced. Yet out of this failed marriage, I have a beautiful daughter who has inspired me to find a better way, live a fuller life. Certainly, feelings of restlessness often sneak up on me when I least expect them. I find that my internal timing mechanism telling me it is "time to move"; however, I feel optimistic, rather than pressured. Rather than surrendering automatically to these feelings, I recognize that I now want to make choices that reflect the things I value, that these rules are no longer working for me. I can see them more clearly than ever.

I think what is most important is to feel my life and share it with the people I love. I feel blessed to be able to see and learn a new way.

I Will Not Be Fooled

Roy was a seeker after truth. This is a key aspect in his search for meaning to his life. He has relied more on reason than faith in his life and is intolerant of people who he thinks lie to him. Sometimes he is thought of as aloof and judgmental when he questions other people's thoughts or actions. Many times his questions are designed to clarify the facts but they are perceived as attacks. He often doesn't realize that some people are intimidated by him.

Rules To Live By:
1. Don't say anything wrong or misleading.
   Give credit to others. Distrust people who don't.
2. Generally trust people, but verify. Be quick to lose trust and assign motives if they are false.
3. Always seek the truth.
4. Don't play mind games, and deflate and interfere with people who try to do this with you.
5. Don't place blame; find the answer.
6. Don't be in the lead; be second. It is easy to be fooled in the lead. Second place allows you to reflect.
7. Only be close to independent people. Dependent people are more likely to try to fool you.
8. I want to be right.
9. I have a strong need to be fair.
10. I don't trust compliments.

I grew up with the profoundly strong father and an irrationally weak mother. I loved my mother and she showed me unconditional love, but I didn't respect her. I loved my father but was afraid of him at times. He was normally aloof but at key times showed me he loved me. My father would often amaze me as a child. I would tell him something I had learned, usually about history, current events, or politics, and he would explain what had really happened. It would be immediately clear that he understood the real story behind the façade; I aspired to be as wise as I saw him.

As I grew up, I was drawn to the clarity and logic of the scientific method and knowledge, areas in which I excelled. I found this an area with a community of people interested in understanding truth and reality with both passion and awe, but also without much chicanery. I was also fascinated by the paranormal and by religion. I read widely about both and visited several religious temples and communities, both Western and Eastern. I was immediately suspicious of belief systems that had the one and only truth. I eventually came to believe that none of the formal religions were more than wise teaching and mythology. My current views are closest to Deist. The paranormal was very exciting, but the more I read over the years, the less reason I found to believe. I eventually ended up being a skeptic and became an active community member of the local skeptic's society.

I have always been in love with knowledge and thinking. I have found many areas of knowledge interesting. I have been involved in many areas of technology. My experience and knowledge has sometimes amazed people and been very valuable in my career. I have a desire to know as much as possible both in the world and in my workplace. This can interfere with my personal and professional life as it reduces the time I can spend with my family and my work objectives.

I hate dishonesty. As a seeker after truth, I have run into many people who have deliberately tried to deceive me. I am very suspicious of salesmen and typically think of them as being guilty until proven innocent. I am not a good salesman myself and this is a necessary aspect of any job. For the last few years, I have been in upper-middle management and recognize I need to change this to be more effective. I am afraid of being in a leadership role because of not wanting to be fooled, knowing that I cannot help but be *fooled sometimes. I am uneasy with the responsibility of high leadership, knowing I will sometimes be wrong and may make a serious mistake.*

It is hard for me to relax and lose control. Being relaxed makes me vulnerable and easier to deceive. I don't trust compliments for similar reasons. I tend to be attracted to and to love independent people who I think are less likely to deceive me. Emotions are difficult for me because they are less objective and fact-based. My tendency to over-intellectualize my feelings can undermine my intimate relationships.

It's Important To Be Reasonable

Dick was considered by many to be a levelheaded husband, manager, and community figure. He was considerate in his requests of others and often gave precedence to their needs over his own.

At work, he was known as a solid and competent manager who was limited by his inability to stretch his staff. Dick felt that he had reasonable expectations of his people. He was not unwilling to permit performance that was sub-par nor did he demand they rise above it. He often would take on extra work to keep them from being overworked. He also was too agreeable with people's reasons for not completing assigned projects.

At home, he was better at compromising than setting boundaries. He gained approval by making others' lives easier rather than greater.

Rules To Live By:
1. Every decision or action of mine must be justified.
2. Be fair in all decisions.
3. People are equal—treat them the same.
4. There are limits to what you can expect of people; after all, we're only human.
5. It's only fair to listen carefully to a person's reasons or excuses for unkept deadlines and agreements.

6. There is always a way to compromise in difficult situations.
7. It's important to be sensitive to people's limitations.
8. A logical approach is best in any situation—emotions have very little to do in good decision making.
9. Only commit to what you know you can do.
10. A reasonable excuse is as good as a result.
11. The best predictor of the future is the past.
12. Always be politically correct.
13. Impulses can be dangerous, careful analysis over time is the best approach to a problem.

From a very early age, I've prided myself on being able to look at complex issues and quickly determine their root cause. I felt that by looking at the total problem, breaking it down into smaller problems, that I could solve the smaller one. This has served me well during my career, and I've built a solid reputation for getting things done and delivering the results.

In fact, I've spent my entire management career coaching people to use this same approach. I've taught them that every problem or situation had a root-a-mentary cause, and that if we found that cause, modified its effect, or removed the cause then the problem, or situation, could be solved.

Emotion has no vote in this situation so don't get too excited, don't take the situation to the extreme boundaries, simply look at the facts, determine or analyze the data. The project is back on track, the company makes money, and life is good. When people engage emotions they lose control of objectivity, and as a result, roll small problems into big ones that no one can solve.

Easy, right? Yeah, that's what I thought too until recently— actually, during a seminar covering this very material. What I discovered, quite frankly, shocked me. It cut to the core of the very fiber I hold so important. What I've come to realize is that emotions are important facts that we must bring into the equation. If we don't we're practicing the strongest method of reason possible!

By cutting out the emotional factor, we've limited the possibility on only one "logical and reasonable" conclusion. If everyone doesn't arrive at the same conclusion as ours, then they simply didn't follow or understand the facts! Or worse, they're illogical and unreasonable people. What worse form of control can possibly exist? You've set the boundaries, determined the parameters and ultimately the decision, one that agrees with yours! The ultimate puppet master.

Now, I'm not suggesting we throw out the facts and discount logic, but I am suggesting that emotions are facts too, and when they are in the equation, you just may not reach that same safe answer as the best approach.

I'm Not Worthy

Tom has spent his life being good, but never good enough. He is a capable manager who enjoys seeing his staff do well. When faced with the challenge for him to really excel, however, he holds back and lets others take the lead. He knows he's innovative and creative, but allows others to push their ideas first. This allows his team to get credit, which is a help to development and morale. It also keeps him from getting the credit he deserves, which damages his morale and self-confidence.

Socially, he is well-liked in that others feel his genuine interest in them. His feelings of not being worthy affect his relationships in how he chooses partners. He picks not from whom he wants most but from whom he feels worthy of.

Rules To Live By:
1. Never speak up unless you know you're right.
2. Always make a splash to make up for the fact that you're not good enough as you are.
3. Be nice.
4. Go out of your way for people who are more worthy than you, even to the point of compromising your own values.

5. Never give up.
6. Let others walk on you.
7. Avoid confrontation.
8. Don't let others know who you really are.

I'm very tenacious, and don't give up easily. I understand well concepts for quality and improvement because I've always looked for ways to do things better. It just seems natural to me that one would continually strive to improve oneself. That's probably why stuff like the "7 Habits of Highly Effective People" and all that I've learned and am learning through Life Success Seminars makes so much sense to me.

I've also learned to be very observant even of subtle details and work out very comprehensive solutions. I think I surprise people sometimes because I sit very quietly and seem like I'm not participating and then, seemingly out of nowhere, I come up with innovative ideas and solutions. I also am able to let others get credit and feel good about it, which has helped me as a manager, and I enjoy seeing others excel.

I'm also quite the survivor! Through all of this I've also felt like I've got something really special to share, and a real ability to make a difference in the world, but I wouldn't take chance. I often hide my "greatness," if I can be so bold. I also find that I'm seldom satisfied with myself or with others.

I guess in some ways it's served me well because I'm very tenacious, and for some reason I've found that I don't always need recognition for a job well done, although I've also accepted recently that I love recognition! I also have pretty much removed the word "can't" from my vocabulary.

Growing up, I don't ever remember being encouraged, unless, perhaps, to conform, but criticism was plentiful whenever I did something "bad," like saying a "bad" word (when I was kid, if I said "fart" instead of "passed gas" that was a bad word), committing some sort of "sin" (very Catholic family).

I remember once (at maybe six or seven) being caught by my father under the covers with my hands down my pants—I'd hear "you should be ashamed of yourself" or "you're a bad boy." When I'd come home happy with B's on my report card I'd be chastised for not getting A's.

I remember another time being very proud of myself for mowing the lawn without being told to do so. I told my dad, "I mowed the lawn today!" and his reply was, "Yeah, but you didn't rake up the clippings." I can still feel the wind being sucked from my sails. It happened over and over. I strived for something but had no model, because pretty much everyone was criticized (except maybe priests and nuns). I still get the criticism and no confidence votes from my parents—even when I excel.

As I look back, I see the results. I always got good grades, maintained a B+ average from grade school through college but never got straight A's. I'd always be good, but not the best. In school plays, I'd get a pretty good part, but never the lead. When I had girlfriends, I always felt like I had to "settle" and often didn't date the girl I really wanted to. That was true even of my marriage.

I guess it was more important for me to protect myself from criticism than to take a chance. As long as I "did good" and kept a low profile, even though I didn't get praise, I didn't get criticized either. At least that way I could maintain a sort of secret self-esteem.

Interestingly, as I think about it, I still feel myself tense up whenever I think somebody is going to criticize me, and I have a really hard time accepting praise.

As a kid, I was rather devious. I'd do things to outsmart my teachers and parents that they never even knew about but that would make me feel somewhat superior. For example, I would devise well thought-out plans for skipping school—I'd let my teacher know in advance that I would need to be excused and that a note would be forthcoming, then I'd forge a letter from my mother and present it. The teacher would think that I was being responsible when really it was all a scam.

I also found myself becoming a bit of a petty thief, feeling good about getting away with it. I probably stole several hundred times, as a kid and never got caught. I guess these things could be seen as rewards, but right now, they feel like costs, because there's a big price in the guilt.

I also didn't reach my potential, so I'd never be satisfied with my results—there was always something better out there. In relationships, I'd eventually start identifying all of my partner's shortcomings and see in other women the things that I wanted that my partner didn't possess. Every time I moved on it would be the same thing and I'd never be satisfied. Nobody was good enough once I got to know them.

I'd never really put out the extra effort to be first because I knew that even first wasn't good enough, so why bother. So, I'd wallow in my misery. I'd see others getting recognition for achievements that I "knew" I could easily do, but I wouldn't do anything about it.

To this day, I don't ask questions in class (unless I know the group very well) because I'll be afraid what I say or ask is somehow wrong or shameful.

When I was in relationships (not just with girls, but with new friends as well), I always felt like I had to make overtures and big splashes because I wasn't good enough to be part of the group, or a good boyfriend, if I didn't do big things to compensate for my unworthiness.

I'd also choose women who were needy, because I've developed into a very good caregiver and would thrive on giving and being needed. Then, when I ran out of splash or got tired of giving, the relationship would often fail because I'd be worn out from having to work so hard and get resentful.

I'd also often be overly nice to try to compensate, even when I wasn't being treated fairly. I have a hard time confronting uncomfortable situations because inside I think I feel like I'm really the one who's at fault no matter what the situation. I still feel like I have the potential to change the world, but I take my chances very carefully.

I always felt like an outsider, like nobody really knew me. If I let people know who I really was then certainly they would have rejected me. I'd be in a room full of people and feel all alone. It wasn't until recently that I started putting myself out there, being vulnerable, and actually experiencing real intimacy.

The World Revolves Around Me

Teri and Tina were identical twins in appearance but thought of as opposites in personality. When Teri entered a room, she was self-conscious, seemingly to a fault. She thought everyone in the room was watching her. Because of this, she was terrified to make a mistake and thus kept to herself.

Tina, on the other hand, also thought everyone in the room was watching her. She reveled in the attention. When it seemed she wasn't getting enough she would become louder, or funnier, or whatever it took.

The only real difference between them was their enjoyment of attention. They both thought that everything that happened was about them. If someone laughed, the laughter was because of something they had done or said. They both felt that people were hanging on their every word, one thought in admiration, the other with the fear of ridicule.

Rules To Live By:
1. Other people are always watching me.
2. Everything that happens is about me.
3. Other people are here to notice me, and it bothers me if they don't.

4. I listen to others to find a way to talk about me.
5. My thoughts and ideas should always be heard.
6. When we are talking about you, I'm still thinking about me.
7. I am always conscious of myself, my thoughts, my feelings.
8. I take other people's comments personally.
9. If I make a mistake, everyone will notice.
10. I think most about how things affect me.

Teri is aware of the strengths she has gained from being this way:

Because I have been more of an observer, I am able to learn a lot about people and what is or is not acceptable just by watching everyone. My shyness enabled me to seem quiet and nice to most people, and I became a good listener.

It has been important for me to be this way because I am so terrified of making a mistake and being ridiculed and rejected that I sometimes felt paralyzed. Being quiet kept me safe.

The price I have paid is that I have had a hard time making new friends. I often appear to be aloof which in turn makes me seem very unapproachable. I wind up with very few friends and often feel alone, even in a crowd."

Tina says:

My strengths are that I am very outgoing and personable. I am not afraid to say exactly what I think, especially if it brings any attention my way. I am able to show more self-confidence than I actually have, so most people view me as having it "all together." I have a lot of courage and have accomplished much, including owning my own businesses. I am a very strong woman and people admire me for my courage. I am also very funny and have a good sense of humor.

It is important for me to be this way because I love to be the center of attention. I am in my element when all eyes are on me. I feel most secure when I am 'center stage.'

The price I have paid is that some people find me to be obnoxious and are turned off by my behavior. If I am not getting attention, I realize just how lonely I am in a crowd. When I am afraid or feeling vulnerable, I bury it under humor or behind a facade of self-confidence and arrogance. Therefore I don't get my needs met. Most people don't know me very well and miss seeing my strong sense of compassion and kindness.

I Am Smarter Than You

Steve was smarter than many around him. He was convinced that this was his unique contribution to his relationships at work and at home. Without realizing it, he had also developed a sense of superiority that came across as arrogance.

People were attracted by his confidence and quick problem-solving ability, but they wanted more of who he was and how he felt. He had also learned over time that he could take shortcuts to solutions that often left others behind. He couldn't understand why people were upset with this, and assumed it was jealousy.

His ability to listen was also clouded by his drive to solve other people's problems. Ultimately, he was a poor partner in professional and social relationships.

Rules To Live By:
1. I am never wrong.
2. Your ideas are building blocks for mine.
3. Always correct other people's mistakes.
4. If I appear wrong—you don't understand what's right.
5. You like me for what I know.
6. The more I know the more you'll like me.
7. You'll like me best if I fix your problems.
8. I listen to find out what you don't understand so I can tell you what I do understand.
9. My intelligence is what makes me special.
10. I size people up quickly; if they don't measure up, I discount or ignore them.

I like finding unusual or difficult situations that others have failed at. These seem like the best opportunities to shine. I am constantly looking for ways to improve whatever surrounds me. If there's a better way to do something, I want to do it.

I like driving teams to find a performance level beyond what they thought they could do. In any situation, I want to be the one with the best solution in the quickest time. Because I'm already looking to improve the environment I'm in, I often can anticipate what's needed and be ready before it's asked for.

I learned early on that being smart was the best way for me to get approval. Sports were okay for exercise and fun, but if you wanted to be special, academics was the place to excel. This was something that came naturally to me so I didn't find it a problem. I have always loved learning and have a deep sense of curiosity about the world around me.

It was only later that I noticed the price I was paying. I have a hard time listening to people without trying to solve their problems. My wife is an intelligent woman who can solve her own issues. Sometimes she just wants to talk about her day; she doesn't need me to fix her.

I also notice that I am so busy thinking that I have a hard time noticing what I'm feeling. For a long time, I felt like Spock—a logical person but not a whole man. It wasn't clear to me for a long time that I hid in my thoughts. Thinking was familiar and safe; it was an easy place to hide.

I Need To Justify My Existence

Beth identifies with many of the previously mentioned "ways of being." She too, wanted to be liked, grew up feeling unworthy, fearing that she would make a mistake, always feeling the need to be in control and to fit in. What Beth now realizes is that all of these things were part of her rules to live by in order to support her intention of *"I need to justify my existence."* Discovering her intention was a wake-up call and a powerful realization for Beth. Looking back to see how the pieces of her life fit together and how she got and supported that intention has been a freeing and yet sometimes painful journey.

Rules To Live By:

1. I am not worthy.
2. I prove my worth by accomplishing things, so it's important to stay busy.
3. Always look like I know what I am doing; never show any fear or uncertainty.
4. Looking good is better than feeling good.
5. Be in control.
6. Be perfect—judge everything I do as not being good enough.
7. Don't make mistakes; people will think I am not capable.
8. Do anything/everything to please others.
9. It's important that others like me.
10. Don't rock the boat.
11. Pretend things are OK, even when they are not.
12. Don't let others really 'know' me because they won't like what they see.

I grew up in a large family, the sixth born in a family of eight. One of the benefits of growing up in a large family is that you are already "part of a group," a group where you should feel the warmth of love and acceptance. Although I came to understand that and feel that as an adult, I spent much of my childhood feeling lonely, scared, and fearful. Somehow, out of all those kids, my mother and I seemed to have the most contentious relationship. I didn't seem to be able to do anything to please her, and one of my earliest memories as a very young child is having her tell me that she wished I had never been born and that the family would have been better off without me.

Coinciding with this message from my mother, my older siblings teased me by telling me I was really adopted and, if I didn't behave, I would be sent back to the orphanage. At some level, I'm sure I knew this wasn't true because it would have been ludicrous to be adopted into a family that already had so many children! But, instead of asking my parents if this were really true, I just set about "justifying my existence" so I could stay, so I would be accepted and loved. (I remember being somewhat afraid that if I reminded them of this fact that they actually might send me back!)

Another element of my family was that there was active alcoholism, although as a child I was not aware that this was a contributing factor to the chaos and tension that I felt. No one ever talked about the alcoholism and it was an unwritten family rule that it was not something you spoke about. In fact, we spent a lot of time "managing" our environment and pretending that things were just fine. To the outside world, we had to "look" like the perfect family and not draw attention to any problems. People like us just didn't have problems. So there was a high value on "looking good" and denying reality. I became very adept at "looking good," no matter how I felt. At the same time, there were some very positive messages received and a strong sense that we were all expected to do big and important things in our lives, the most important being a sense of "giving back" to society.

During most of my childhood, I just tried to "get along" and not be noticed. I tried to fly beneath the radar screen so as not to attract the kind of attention that might get me "sent back." I was overweight (in my family, you just didn't say fat) and in early grade school suffered from a stuttering problem. I wasn't very popular and didn't have many friends. I was a pretty good student although I never thought of myself as being very talented. I spent a lot of time comparing myself to others and could always find someone cuter, smarter, skinnier, etc. among my siblings and classmates.

As I got a little older, I did find my niche in sports and discovered I was a pretty good athlete—something that my other sisters couldn't claim. For the first time, I felt that I had found something that I could do well and therefore, I could contribute to the family value that it was important to "accomplish things."

In my early teens, I also discovered that I didn't like the feeling of loneliness and not fitting in. I can almost remember the moment that I "decided" that I was going to have an outgoing personality. My rationale was that no one was going to be attracted to me, so if I wanted to have friends and feel that I belonged, I had better get myself in gear and start being friendly. This was probably one of the greatest gifts or boosts that I gave myself. People who know me today would hardly believe there was ever a time when I wasn't outgoing—it's just a part of who I am.

I left for college fearful of what lay ahead. I may have left the chaos at home behind, but I was very confused about life and didn't have a great deal of confidence. I didn't really think I was up to the task but it wasn't OK not to go—after all, that's what was expected of me. After two years, I broke a major family rule when I got married and subsequently dropped out of college. I was thrilled to have found someone who was going to rescue me from this confusion called life and now I didn't have to worry about being safe, or being loved. That little bubble didn't last long when, after two years of marriage, I was divorced with a young son to take care of. In my family, you just DIDN'T get divorced. It is honestly the first time in my life that I went against "public opinion" and stood up for myself! I knew I had made a mistake and, as I looked ahead at a potential life of unhappiness, I knew had to do something!

What I didn't realize then was how important this "breaking the rules" was for me. In spite of people thinking the worst of me, I had found my own voice and a strength I didn't know I had. Believing in myself has served me well through the years. In the beginning, just thinking it was enough—it gave me a newfound courage on which to build my life.

In both my personal life, which includes a remarriage to a wonderful man and raising two equally wonderful children, and in *my professional life, I have accomplished much. I have moved from the desire and drive to 'do great things' in order to fill that empty place inside of me to celebrating the joy that comes from filling my soul with meaningful work and with the people in my life. As is most often the case, I gained much strength from my Way of Being. I learned how to do things and to do them well. I am someone who can be counted on. I care deeply about others and their well-being. My professional career has been spent working in the non-profit/social service field. I believe I am less judgmental because I lived with the pain of feeling judged in my life.*

Today, I have discovered a new intention that reminds me of how I want to live my life, which is in a space of joy, celebration, and connection to others. I can claim my gifts and accomplishments and not feel the need to impress others or pretend to be someone/something I am not. I speak out on issues that I feel passionate about. And I know that others do not always agree with me. I am no longer willing to have someone else's opinion of me be the measure of my worth. I believe in the goodness inside of me and I see the goodness in others. Perhaps it is best summed up as "what you see is what you get"—what people see on the outside, is actually how I FEEL on the inside.

I am enough; I don't need to prove myself.

My New Rules for Living:

1. I am a human being, not a human doing.
2. I appreciate and celebrate my accomplishments.
3. I let my exuberance show.
4. I honor and use my gifts and talents.
5. No one else can make me feel inferior without my permission.
6. I am not perfect; some of my 'mistakes' have also been my greatest gifts for learning and growing.
7. I feel joy in my connection with others and also allow time for myself.
8. I love my sense of humor and sense of fun.

9. I am a giver AND a receiver.
10. I'M IN CONTROL.

Kim considered herself to be a natural leader. She was recognized as having many strong traits, such as confidence, a strong will, and good verbal skills. Other people saw her as controlling and arrogant. She was better at listening to her own ideas than those of her team. She was unable to take criticism constructively and was often defensive during the process. Those around her felt more like her servants than her colleagues.

Kim was a hard worker who occasionally took projects back from her staff if she felt things were behind. She also was a notorious micro-manager.

At home, she acted in a consistent manner. She was confused and angry about why her husband had pulled back in the marriage. He had stopped contributing and was becoming more aloof and distant.

Rules To Live By:
1. I am willing to step up and take the lead, even in chaos.
2. Surrender is a form of weakness; the only way to be safe is to be in control.
3. If you want something done right, do it yourself.
4. If I'm not the leader, I probably won't contribute.
5. People take advantage when I'm vulnerable.
6. If I admit to a mistake people won't believe in me.
7. I sometimes use anger or bully people to get my way.
8. I may also use guilt or withhold affection to be in control.
9. Other people may find me insensitive or rude, but that's their problem.
10. If I need to, I can talk louder or faster to make my point.

There are many times I take control to make sure there are no mistakes. This has taught me that I can do more than I believed I could. I feel more capable to run my world than I was raised to be. I was raised to believe that men are supposed to be in control and women have to live with it.

I also have learned to have more confidence in my abilities. I take more risks than I ever thought I would. Often this is hard on my family who think I take too many risks. I still worry about how they will turn out, but I've done better than I ever expected.

I take control to protect myself from things not getting done, or done right. My husband doesn't worry about details, so I feel that if I don't, we might get in trouble. I especially don't like the feeling of not knowing what's going on. I hate the idea of being blindsided financially, emotionally, or socially.

I guess there was always a feeling in my family that appearances were more important than feelings. We had to look, act, and dress appropriately or Mom would get mad. We had appearances to keep up to maintain our status.

It's hardest to be this way when I take on things I'm not good at. I get frustrated and angry and look for someone to blame it on. I worry a lot and live under a lot of stress. When that happens, I forget about other people's feelings and needs. I may say or do things I'll later regret at these times.

I find myself missing out on enjoying life because I'm so worried about missing something I should have handled. I also find it hard to surrender emotionally; I'm afraid if I let go I might not get control back. This has put a strain on the intimacy in my marriage and creates a wall between us. Sometimes I hate to go out because it takes so much time to get ready; it just doesn't seem worth it.

I Don't Make Mistakes

Franco was conscientious about detail and had been most of his life. He had been a good student in school, in part because of excellent study habits. He was pleased by the grades his study produced, but he had a deeper motivation.

Franco may have been pleased with an "A" but, more than

that, he feared any mistake. His drive was not so much to achieve excellence but to avoid failure.

This carried over to his relationships. He had developed a habit of disclaiming responsibility for problems in the marriage. He also had a difficult time apologizing to his wife when things went poorly. He knew that he was very careful not to make mistakes and justified his finger-pointing with the thought that he was probably right anyway.

Rules To Live By:
1. Take time to do things right.
2. If it's wrong, it's not my fault—I didn't do it.
3. If I did it, you somehow made me do it.
4. When something goes wrong, find out who's at fault first.
5. Don't finalize making a decision until the last moment.
6. After making decisions, second-guess yourself.
7. Safety comes in not making mistakes.
8. No decision at all is better than one that may be wrong.
9. Worry is an important tool to keep oneself alert to possible problems.
10. If something goes wrong that I haven't spent time worrying about, it may be my fault.
11. Never forget a mistake.

I am a second-generation oldest son of migrant workers. My parents worked like dogs to provide food, shelter, and a decent education for my two brothers, my sister, and me. As the eldest, I was the first member of my family to ever go to college. I felt that any time I failed it wasn't just me I was letting down but my whole family. They had worked so hard and paid so many prices that I knew I would never disappoint them.

Looking back, I don't know if college really was harder for me than for others but I know I was driven to study harder and get higher grades than the other students. I didn't have the time for the parties and social life that seemed so important for them.

I went to work after school with the same intense drive that I used at school. I always check and double check my work to make sure it's perfect before I finish a project. In the beginning, this worked really well for me and my manager always felt she could count on me.

It has been eight years since I started here and I now manage the department I started in. Everyone in my family is so proud of me and thinks I am so successful, but I feel like I am about to burn out. I not only check and double check my work but the work of the four people who report to me and the people who report to them. When I find a mistake, I know I can't trust them and become even more thorough in checking up on them. I also give them less work and do more of their job myself.

I am nervous about asking for help because that seems like an admission of failure. My boss still trusts me but has started to push on me to get things done faster but I have run out of hours in the day to make sure it's done right.

I Take the Easy Way Out

Mike was very observant and smarter than people knew. He learned early that life was easier if he didn't risk; then others would lower their expectations of his abilities. He spent most of his life not telling anyone what his goals were because this would expose him.

He found by observing others he could learn the easy way, requiring minimum risk and the feeling of being smarter. Unfortunately, this approach didn't work all the time and many opportunities were missed.

As a result of missing out, he found it easy to second-guess, judge, and ridicule those who had what he had missed. He was strong enough to have his voice heard, not as a leader but as a complainer, unwilling to risk being a leader. The final result was that life was more difficult trying to find the easy way.

Rules To Live By:
1. Don't show your hand.
2. Always figure out the easy way.
3. It's easier to complain than risk.
4. Buck authority; they're the enemy.
5. If you wait long enough, they will see it your way.
6. Blend in.
7. Avoid people who are better than you.

I have learned tremendous patience; I'm willing to wait on the desired outcome. I find that by observing others I learn their strengths and can avoid their mistakes. I am able to set realistic goals and consistently achieve them. I don't take other people's complaints about how I lead personally. I expect them to complain.

I have been this way to stay safe. I am in control. I don't have to depend on others and people don't know what to expect from me. It also allows me to avoid conflict. It may be only for a moment and sometimes what I avoid disappears forever. I also don't like to say "no," because that feels like conflict to me.

The price I've paid is missed opportunities. I feel I got a late start in life. I sometimes wonder what I could have done if I had gotten after it when I was younger.

Sometimes I hold back because I fear I'm not as smart as someone else. I never find out when I don't take risks. I still feel a lot of stress about making timely decisions. I also make it hard for others to help when I don't let them in on what I'm committed to. When I need their assistance, especially in a new or difficult situation, I find I may have lost their trust.

I Must Fit In

Lidia was the child of Ukrainian immigrants. They had been through several countries on their way to the USA. When she was ten, she went to her first day of school in Rochester, NY. When she arrived in her classroom, she was scared. It was December and everyone already knew each other. They all stared at her.

She noticed that nobody else looked like her. Lidia had long braids and coke-bottle-thick glasses. Worst of all, her mother had her wear her uniform from the last place she went to school, and the kids in New York wore street clothes. She felt she stood out in the most painful way.

Because she had already studied many of the things her classmates were learning, she was allowed to skip a grade. That afternoon, some of the kids followed her home from school. They taunted her about how she looked and threatened to beat her up. They asked her who she thought she was for skipping a grade.

She knew they didn't like her because she was smart and also because she looked different than they did. That day she vowed to do her best to blend in and not stand out. She decided that it was dangerous to appear different than others.

She also began to believe that if others perceive you as too smart, you won't have any friends. In many subtle ways she still hides her gifts even though her conscious desire is to be in front and leading.

Rules to Live By
1. Listen carefully before speaking.
2. Being different isn't acceptable.
3. If you want to change things, go slowly and get the group consensus.
4. Be cautious in dress and mannerisms.
5. Don't challenge the status quo.
6. Be careful not to offend.
7. Don't let people know if you're smarter than they are.
8. Let others take the lead.

My greatest strengths have evolved as a result of choosing my way of being. Since I hid my gifts so well as a child, I am very adept at looking for how others do that too. I even look for signs of it in people who appear not to be hiding their gifts. It has resulted in my discovering the buried talents in the people with whom I interact. This has been especially useful in my work as an executive leadership coach in business arenas and in my psychotherapy practice.

I listen well and often "hear" even that which is unspoken. Because of this gift, I am able to help people see/feel a bigger picture and to enlarge their view of their genius and goals. Since I have a high need for affiliation, I don't tend to intimidate people. This has been a plus. It enables me to provide even difficult information without damaging the relationship.

I am also very diplomatic. This too has been a beneficial skill. I am able to give honest feedback without diminishing the person. I genuinely see what is possible and think strategically so I can assist the person to find their way to a better quality of life and work.

I am interested in looking at people deeply and rarely judge someone by their appearance or my initial impression. Intimacy is of great value to me, and I enjoy being authentic and seek relationships that explore those qualities. Therefore, I am a good friend, and in professional circles, I am trusted and respected.

It has been important to be this way because it has allowed me to develop relationships that add to the joy and learning in my life. I enjoy sharing the journey with others, and it is delightful to have many people in my circle.

It has been gratifying to be a transformational influence in peoples' lives. I am very interested in illuminating the potential of finding the gifts that life challenges offer.

Having good relationships with people adds to my self-esteem and sense of mastery in life. When I was a child, I worried about being alone and without friends. Now I know how to make and keep good friends.

There has been a price I have paid in my "way of being." I have stayed in relationships that were not working well for me because I could see the person's gifts. Rather than focusing on my true feelings, I worked on sustaining the relationship even though *in the end it would have been better for me to move on.*

And there has been a loss in being completely spontaneous. I temper my outrageous and ostentatious impulses. Most of the time I am more invested in being appropriate than in expressing my inner clown.

I'm Uniquely Special

Allan had always had a feeling of being special. He had grown up feeling frustrated that other people couldn't see it. He thought it was true but secretly wondered if maybe it wasn't.

He was intolerant of people who were brash or egotistical for no apparent reason and subtly sought ways to deflate them. It felt as if they were taking the special spot without having earned it.

In time, he grew less and less subtle and appeared to others to be judgmental, arrogant, and brutally honest. He had struggled with justifying his "specialness" until he developed a skill set that was unique enough to be noticed by others.

He developed a talent of keen insight and had learned to use it in helpful ways. He was concerned about other people and showed it in ways that highlighted his unique differences. But after he had convinced others of his unique gifts, he still kept the barriers between them.

Rules To Live By:
1. Always find the unique point of view.
2. Find the unusual solution to difficult problems.
3. Listen to others to find a way to promote yourself.
4. Gifts should be impressive first, and heartfelt second.
5. Don't let people know your weaknesses; special people aren't weak.
6. Letting other people know about their flaws will keep them from seeing yours.
7. Stay distant and aloof; don't let people get too close—they might see a flaw.
8. Take on the projects that others are afraid of.
9. When everything is in chaos, take the lead to save things.
10. Sometimes you have to create chaos to show people how great and special your leadership skills are.

I have always loved situations that would bring out my best. I don't mind the pressure or the occasional failure as long as I get a shot at greatness. I learned from my father that 95% of people would be herd animals and never really think for themselves. I was determined not to be one of those 95%.

I have always sought to broaden my thinking. I look for unique solutions or applications that others haven't tried. I have also learned to trust my intuition to find solutions to issues that linear thinking won't solve. The intuitive ability along with the risk-taking gives me the ability to get past people's defenses to address deep-seated issues. Early on I learned to challenge commonly-held beliefs that often hold others back.

It was important for me to be this way to show I was special. I was convinced that I didn't want to be a herd creature. There was a clear understanding of what constituted the best way to be. I felt that I was expected to be creative, talented, polite, intelligent, and honest. There was an assumption that I would do all this in a humble and unassuming way.

Much like the Lone Ranger, I would be heroic, save the day, then disappear without a trace. I was taught to eschew that which was common in thought, humor, music, and effort. I thought this is what I was supposed to be to get love, acceptance, and approval.

The cost was in losing me. I find it impossible to try to be special and be genuine at the same time. Each time I speak, it has to be a deep thought. When I'm with others, there is an underlying attempt to impress them. To be special has required a feeling of being elitist. If I was in the 5%, then you were probably in the 95%.

I found myself constantly trying to fix people. (What better way to let them know they don't quite measure up?) My relationship at home is at its worst when I try to fix my wife. I find the need to be special also creates distance between us. I am always subtly trying to set myself apart. I do this so I will be noticed as different, and so I will get all the credit.

It has only been recently that I have started to have peace with this need to be special. Though I have been aware of it for a few years, I have lately become aware that underneath it was a fear that I was quite ordinary. With that thought in mind, I found myself looking to see what my real gifts were under the fear. I was hoping to find the happy ending, the pot of gold at the end of the rainbow. I was secretly expecting that the fear would be an illusion and that I really was uniquely special under it all. Peace came differently than I thought it would; it arrived with the knowing that I was really ordinary in many ways and that is good enough. I don't need to be better than anyone to be fulfilled.

It is important to remember that most of us have more than one "*way of being*." The interplay between your two or three choices will give you a more precise picture.

Once again, I want to remind you that personality comes from the Greek word for mask. When we talk about the aspects of personality, we are talking about the elements that make up our masks. Another way to think about it is that these are the bricks that make up the wall that keeps you separate; separate from those that you love and separate from truly knowing your own unique talents and gifts. This is not who you are; this is what you do that keeps you from being truly known.

Who's Holding Your Strings?

Think of the "way of being" as an agreement. This agreement may have been made between you and somebody else, or with God, or with yourself. It is helpful to know with whom you are keeping the agreement. Does the other person know what the agreement is?

The list of rules is also a set of agreements. These agreements are about how you will act. If you live around Nancy, she agrees not to upset you by making waves. She probably hasn't told you this. She upholds her end of the agreement without your knowing there is one. You may like waves, you may want to know her opinions, but you are bound by an agreement that you can't know about.

Each person she has that agreement with (which in this case is everyone she meets) is holding the end of a string that ties her down. She hands them the end of a string that they don't know they are holding. To her it feels as if she is beholden to keep her agreement with each person she meets. We are the unwitting accomplices that have her feeling stuck.

Things to remember

1. **These are a part of what we do, not who we are.**

2. **Many of our greatest strengths and talents were developed because we have been this way.**

3. **They become problems when we automatically apply them in inappropriate situations.**

4. **They are signs of our strength and creativity.**

7

The Hidden Benefits

There are three major stumbling blocks that impede people in telling the unspoken truth. First, they can't believe that they have the power of intention. It seems unbelievable that they could have the ability to choose a life, especially for those who choose at such a young age. As a society, we are much more comfortable with cause and effect or blame than responsibility and free choice.

Second, many people's self-image is built on a foundation of believing that their personality or mask is who they really are, when in fact they are different than their perceptions. They fear digging under the surface and into the shadow because they may discover flaws that may affect their self-image.

The third difficult aspect of the truth is that all our behaviors are rewarding to us. Hidden in our behavior, no matter how painful, there is a reward. No one likes the sound of this and it seems wrong on the surface. I have often heard people ask, "If I have the power to choose a life why would I choose this?" We are so aware of the price

we pay for our choices that it seems inconceivable that there
a benefit. What could anyone possibly get out of failed relationships
or a short-circuited career? Why would any of us bring those things
on ourselves when they obviously cause so much grief?

It's hard to see the reward we get in our situation but often
easier to see in someone else. Take for instance a hypochondriac,
someone who acts sick when they aren't. If you were to ask him
what his reward is he would say that there is none. He is miserable
and may well die soon. If you have ever known such a person, you
may believe him at first, but in time you notice that he gets a benefit
out of pretending to be sick. Perhaps he gets attention or sympathy;
maybe he just wants to avoid responsibility for some area of his life.
He is well aware of the price he pays—the doctor bills, the
medication, the symptoms, and the eventual disbelief by family and
friends.

What is missed is the reward. This isn't surprising because to
acknowledge the rewards would be the end of the behavior. It would
require an admission and an understanding that the whole behavior
was created for a hidden benefit. It just wouldn't work to say to a
friend, "I'll pretend to be sick if you'll pretend to love me." We can't
afford to be aware of our rewards until we are ready to give up the
behavior!

It is at this point that I hear, "Yes, but hypochondriacs are sick
people. I really don't want this; I am ready to give it up." What
people are usually ready to give up is the price. It is the rare
individual who can see how the price they pay and the reward they
receive are connected. It is hard to see the cause and effect
relationship of our own behavior.

I knew a man I'll call Bob. Bob had decided at an early age that
the one thing he couldn't live without was his father's approval.
Bob's dad was a successful entrepreneur who valued hard work and
had a profitable business. By the time Bob was in his forties he had
a very successful business and knew that much of what he had

accomplished he had done out of respect for his father's wishes. What he really wanted to focus on now was his relationship. Bob was on his second marriage and it was on the rocks.

His wife had told him he was disconnected from her. He rarely shared his feelings and they spent little time together. He was also concerned that his children had grown distant and seemed upset with him. Bob had decided that what he needed to do was to get in touch with his feelings and become more open. He thought that if he could become a more feeling person that he would be able to resolve these issues. Bob thought the problems stemmed from his being somewhat closed. While it was true that he wasn't very open, he never thought that his distance from his family was the price he was paying for his success at work. He was aware that he had decided to try to win his father's approval through his achievements but was unaware of the price he paid for it. All the hours he spent at the office were hours he spent away from his family. He had managed to compartmentalize the two and failed to see the connection.

I was sharing this with a friend who was also highly driven. He said he had the same issue when his young daughter gave him a sobering wake-up call. They were on their way from a family funeral where the deceased had his ashes spread over a lake. My friend's daughter was curious on the way home as to why they had done this. Her mother explained that the person had always loved that lake and that it was his favorite place. She further said that some people have a place that they love more than any other and they spend as much time there as they can. When it becomes time to find a final resting place, they request to be left in that spot forever. After a moment's thought, the daughter replied that when daddy died they would probably spread his ashes at the office. Her words felt like a dagger to my friend's heart. He knew he would have to change or pay the price Bob was paying.

Bob probably had many similar wake up calls from his family

but wasn't ready to wake up. He wasn't ready to get closer to his family because it may have cost him the reward he was getting at the office. When he started work on this, he was ready to try anything, anything that didn't interfere with his work. Bob couldn't see how those two parts went hand in hand because to see how his trying for his father's approval was costing him his family's love meant he would have had to make a choice that he wasn't ready to make.

Bob didn't want to pay the bill after he had already eaten the meal. Even though he wasn't clear about his hidden benefits, he was aware of the prices he pays. It's like using a credit card. We often use it to satisfy an impulse in a moment, one that is soon forgotten. Unfortunately, even though he may have forgotten what he received as a benefit, the bill still comes with a demand for payment. The reward comes first and is often quickly forgotten, but the bill comes every month and can be a source of constant aggravation, especially if he has forgotten what he gained in the first place.

Upon noticing the price they pay, people prefer to place blame outside themselves. They blame their problems on their parents or circumstances outside their control. In our society, we have ample support for doing just that. If we are seeking to place blame, this is a convenient solution.

If we are seeking to change, this behavior is misguided. Some people are genuinely dealing with issues outside their control. Most of us are avoiding responsibility for our actions because we don't understand they stem from our choices. We make the choices that are rewarding to us in ways we don't acknowledge or can be consciously aware of, because we haven't yet turned our attention to look in those places. Our behaviors, both constructive and destructive, are rewarding to us. These rewards are why we do what we do.

Think for a moment of one behavior you consistently do. Maybe you avoid confrontation, procrastinate, act self-righteous or.... Somewhere inside, you are convinced that there is a benefit to doing that no matter what the price.

Consider some of the stories we've looked at so far. Kate was acting invisible. When she knew she had to take on the mantle of leadership to achieve her dreams, she thought she was ready to become visible. Thinking it wasn't enough. Neither is wishing, hoping, or positive thinking it enough. Kate needed to dig down and find the reward for being invisible. Even though she knew the concept about reward and price, she still thought that her "invisibility" was the right way to be and that others should try it as well. She resisted looking for a hidden ulterior motive. When she did, she discovered that it was a response to her self-image of being small in a large world.

Or think back to the young manager who procrastinated when he needed to deliver bad news. He sometimes saw that as a character flaw over which he had no control, and other times saw it as being kind because he didn't want to hurt people's feelings. He had a terrible struggle in finding that he was rewarded by getting people to like him.

Even those people who start to *accept responsibility* for who they are find it easier to claim the roots of their behavior, while stopping short of seeing the current rewards for their actions. It is easier to say they now do what they do because it's a habit, or by finding a convenient justification for what they do.

This can seem bewildering at times; especially when you start to grasp that your intention creates your results and yet you are clearly getting something that you don't *think* you want. This is when it's time to dig into the shadows of your life to see what hidden reward you might be getting. The cause of some confusion is that even though your intention leads to your results, every result is not what you intended but the price you pay to get what you intended. Bob didn't intend to be separate from his family. Separation from his family was the price he paid for his success. It was a consequence of his intention.

Take a look at the story of Nancy and my responses to her. She had read this far and replied as follows:

So I am a person with a weight problem. I lost 28 pounds two years ago and in this past year have managed to gain nearly all of it back. I make resolutions, promises to me; I even manage to do fairly well for a while until I sabotage myself again.

Even during the time of my weight loss, I had problems. I would lose two or three pounds only to gain back one or two or sometimes even more. So in reality, the year I lost 28 pounds, I really lost at least 50, only I re-gained and re-lost many pounds over and over again.

I have tried logic, guilt, support groups, pills, EVERYTHING, and here I am still fat and miserable.

I felt so much better, lighter, younger, sexier, and more self confident, and worthier than I had in years. Yet, in less than a year, I had managed to regain the weight and with it the loss of many of those great feelings. I now feel lethargic, older, less self-confident, unattractive, unworthy, ashamed, and embarrassed. I am obsessed with the misery I have created, and I feel so helpless. It is a feeling not much different than that craving for a drink that I used to have constantly.

My mother and all of her siblings were overweight, and so are most of my cousins, though a few have managed to keep themselves fit (four out of 28). So while I know that the tendency for being obese is hereditary, four of these people have managed to stay thin.

1. *So while I may whine about my weight, I know that it is my intention to be heavy because this is my result. It makes sense that this intention is unconscious, and different than what I say I want; because I say I want to be thin, and here I am ... fat.*

2. *My long-term pattern has been for instant gratification. When I am afraid or unhappy, or feeling anything negative, I go for food because it is a comfort. There are other things I am sure I do that you may notice more easily, so please help*

me with this.

3. *I haven't figured out what the reward is except for the instant gratification. And I get to feel sorry for myself. I guess I get to remain safe. As much as I say I want to be in a relationship, there is still some fear. And the weight will scare off any potential partner.*

4. *It pisses me off because all of this is my fault and I seem to only be able to direct my power the wrong way. I hate being responsible for this. (Stopping to cry now.)*

Nancy, you are absolutely correct in linking your results to your intentions. Becoming aware that your intentions are the cause of your results is the first step to reclaiming control of your life. It is an oversimplification, however, to say that everything that happens to you is something that you somehow intended.

Many things that are long-time patterns are a result of what you intended. In your case, I think you may be mistaking the price you pay for the intention itself. In your point #2, your desire for comfort is probably closer to what you want. You clearly identified food as your means of achieving it. Weight and the emotional baggage that comes with it may be the prices you pay for finding comfort in food, or it may be a technique you use to find comfort.

Let me explain. One possibility is that you didn't intend to be overweight; it's that you had to pay the price for comfort through eating. You also likely have a genetic disposition for holding weight that aggravates this situation. It seems possible that you would rather be comfortable than thin. In the past, you found comfort in drink and lived with the price of that. When you tired of the price of drinking, you found sobriety. Unfortunately, letting go of drinking didn't mean letting go of the intention to be comfortable, which you now know you find in food.

You then clearly state why food brings comfort and what the weight keeps you comfortable from—relationships and the fear of being hurt again. Finally, you conclude with berating yourself for not being able to change it. Unfortunately, this self-condemnation only leads to less self-esteem, which leads to greater insecurity and a renewed need for comfort. I will speak more on that in the next chapter.

When Nancy saw the chapter on intention, she wrote:

My reason to live, I learned, was to be a nice little girl when I was very young and was always looking for approval. There was a time when I was four or five I was trying desperately to be friends with some little girls down the street. I just didn't seem to fit in but with my mother's encouragement to go out and play with those nice little girls—I kept on trying to make friends.

One day, two of the girls told me to close my eyes because they wanted to show me something. When I was instructed to open my eyes, they were "mooning" me. I can still remember that awful feeling of rejection and helplessness. I immediately turned around and walked home, hiding my tears from them. At that moment, I had decided that I had to keep myself safe from being hurt and rejected. I walked away and never spoke of it to my mother, because of my shame and fear that she would know that others viewed me as worthless. Maybe the fear was that she would agree. I became very shy, and found it hard to make friends with children my age.

The next incident that I remember that affected me was when I was around 11; my dad left me. I say "left me" because even though he was walking out on the marriage, I felt that it was me who he walked out on. Again I felt that total feeling of rejection and loneliness. I guess it was then that I decided that I was unacceptable.

Nancy, that was the pebble in the pond. That created the first splash. You saw the events that happened and decided what they meant about you. That belief that you were unacceptable was what caused the ripples that led to your intention to be safe.

Many years later, a woman whom I had known all of my life said to me that she had always felt sorry for me as a child. I was confused, because all things considered, I felt I had had a decent childhood. She said that when she was with us, my poor mother was so busy with my oldest brother (by four years) and my mentally retarded brother, who was older by 18 months, that she barely had time for me. This, along with the fact that my dad worked many hours and was also an alcoholic, made life pretty busy for my mom.

This tells me that from my birth, life was hectic for my mother and that feeling of not being important began almost at once. I know I always felt "less than" and could never be good enough or pretty enough for mom. Many things I have done ever since I can remember have been self-destructive, self-defeating, or very "nice" so "they" would approve of me.

I know that right now I am enforcing my agreements with some very self-destructive behavior, not only in the weight department, but for my career as well. The things I say I want: to lose 30 pounds, be in a loving relationship, and facilitate seminars are the very things I have been working on for the past few years, yet I seem to sabotage myself every time I begin to move forward on any of these dreams.

For the past five years, I have moved forward and gone beyond my wildest expectations of what I could do. I have severed many strings that held me back, yet the same agreements and intentions that I felt I had severed, are the very ones that have me now.

Think of the decision to be safe as your intention. It has all the hallmarks of a very deep desire that is the source of intention. The strings are more like the way you go about being safe. Think of them as the rules you live by that guarantee your safety—rules like "I will always be nice," "I will try to fit in," and "I will always be cute or funny." Each time you break one of those unwritten rules that you live by, you loosen the hold that your "way of being" has on you.

I notice that you have an exceptional grasp of responsibility. You are clear about the influence that your family history played, but you have also claimed credit for being the one who interpreted the meaning of these events. Your father was absent a great deal and your mother was busy with your siblings, yet you understand that you decided what that meant about you, rather than feeling it caused you to be a certain way.

You have clarity about how you devalued your worth as a way to explain the inattention of your parents. You have made efforts to sever the behaviors that have kept you tied down. This tells me you are well on your way to using your intention as a power to assist in fulfilling your dreams.

All of this seems to fit in with the "I want to be liked" pattern I have lived. Since my earliest memories, I have tried to "fit in" and wanted affirmation and approval. The only way I could find my worth and importance was to be liked. I found that when I was funny and did silly things, people seemed to approve of me and like me. Many times, I compromised myself in order to be liked. I hid my feelings and was strong.

When I chose not to argue or protect myself, I ran to the food. My biggest weakness seems to be in food. That is where I learned to find my comfort. This feeling I am sure came to me as well as to most of us, as a small infant. When I was upset or cried, I was fed. Being fed included being held and comforted by my mother. As I grew older, many times food, a treat, was used for a reward. If I were a "good girl," I would get a treat of some sort. So I found comfort in food. I have written this in past tense but it is still clearly in the present for me.

So, because I decided I was unacceptable or unlikable at an early age, the choices I have made (don't make waves, never get angry, etc.) were made so I would be accepted and liked by others. The fact that I sabotage myself and beat myself up are things I do to fulfill an intention that I am unacceptable AND that I have been doing it for so long that my behavior is automatic, as if I had no control over any of it.

I don't think you ever intended to be unacceptable. That seems like a conclusion you came to, based on the circumstances of your life. We commonly try to make sense of our lives by concluding that other people's behavior is based on who *we* are. It takes years to realize that other people—your mother and father, and those little girls who teased you—were treating you the way they did because of who they were, not because of who you were.

If I want to accept responsibility for this behavior, and regain my power, I first must change the agreement that I made with myself as a small child. I think the suggestion of posting my accomplishments in a prominent place is a great one for starters.

Also, I know that when I do certain things daily, I am much less likely to use the self-destructive behaviors. These things include centering, spending some time talking to God, and writing a gratitude list (three good things that happened today and three things I am proud of myself for today). I have come a long way in the "I want to be liked" department, but there is much work to be done there too. I guess my confusion is where do I go from here?? What can I do to cut a string?"

Few of us ever get the clean, decisive victory that we hope for. Occasionally you may see a destructive behavior or pattern of behavior end all at once, just as you did when you decided to stop drinking. Often the behavior may have stopped, never to return, but we may still be struggling with the urges each day.

In time, there may come a day when you realize that the desire is gone and has been gone for some time. Until then, a vigilant approach to hunting down the source of the agreement to be comfortable and challenging the rules for comfort is the most appropriate course. Remember, the bottom line was to be comfortable. Finding comfort in situations that had previously felt risky will take some time and a great deal of conscious practice.

People too often become frustrated after years of effort as they encounter the same obstacles in themselves time and again. I regularly hear of people experiencing huge interpersonal insights that they think will be permanent life-changing events, only to discover that the behaviors that we thought would be gone permanently have returned within moments.

I have heard it explained by the tenacity of habits. It is often said that we are creatures of habit, that to make life a little easier, we have learned to act in an automatic fashion without thinking about what we are doing. After acting automatically, we notice that we have just done something that we promised never to do again.

It seems that at these times, we have some kind of unconscious radar looking ahead of us, that at some level we are deciding if we need to wake up and really think about what we are doing, or whether we can employ one of our habitual behaviors and save ourselves the trouble of being alert. I have read for years that it takes 21 days of acting differently to change a habit; I believe it may take longer for such deeply embedded behavior.

I have also heard that we may, through constant use, wear a kind of "mental rut" in the structure of the brain itself; it may be that the brain has the ability to structure itself to support how we think. That will have to be determined by people more schooled in neurology than I am.

We also may struggle because of the very complexity of the layering and compartmentalizing of our brains and mind. From an experiential point of view, this makes some sense. Often the insights that we have are acted upon only in the context in which we have those insights.

For instance, I was talking with a woman a few years ago who had always felt like an outcast and couldn't figure out why. After some reflection, she realized that she had an attitude of being "better than" and self-righteous. With this insight, she felt she had solved the mystery of how she offended others and she left happy. Shortly, she was puzzled about her relationship at home. Once again, upon reflection, she discovered the same self-righteous behavior. She was an intelligent woman who somehow missed the connection between the behavior with her friends and the way she was at home. This time she was truly resolved to lay this to rest.

I saw her a while later as she struggled to come to grips with an issue at work that, predictably, was the same issue revisited. It was as if a tendency for this behavior was stored inside her in a variety of places that could only be accessed when she was in the appropriate environment. She had to confront this part of her each place it showed up, and in time, she found that the same feelings of self-righteousness were imbedded at different levels. As she became more familiar with herself at deeper levels, she found traces of arrogance hidden in seemingly innocuous behavior.

She noticed, for instance, that she sometime gave gifts with the idea of correcting a person's deficiencies, as a subtle message that there was something wrong with the receiver. Regardless of why change is so hard to achieve and why we seem to have to conquer the same beasts so many times, the truth is that "change ain't for sissies."

Nancy has started to see her behavior is not just a reflection of an early childhood choice, but has realized that her desire to be liked is being made each moment of her life. The rules she lives by aren't habits that she needs to break, but are choices she constantly makes in order to reward herself. The reward she continuously seeks is to show that she is acceptable. In other words, this isn't an old belief she is living out; it is one she remakes each moment. Each moment of each day, she renews her vow to her "way of being." For her this is, "I want to be comfortable and safe."

Her Rules to Live By:
1. Always be nice.
2. Be cute and funny.
3. When I am afraid, hurt, sad, or feel threatened, I run to my safety net—food.
4. When I feel that utter emptiness inside myself, I run to my safety net—food.
5. Food = safety, acceptance and love, so I share, make food and give it as gifts to show love and receive love and acceptance.
6. Don't push yourself too far out of your comfort zone; it's scary out there.
7. I am not good enough, talented enough, smart enough, etc., and never will be; accept unworthiness.
8. When I am emotional, I go unconscious and eat, forgetting all other promises and commitments I have made.
9. Always find fault with my progress.
10. The only way to feel worthy, successful, talented, etc., is to get approval from others.

Through awareness, she has begun the process of changing her intention. She recognizes the rewards she has sought and has decided that she has the power to consciously change. For the last few years, she has committed herself to a new way of being.

Her *New* Rules for Living:
1. Be honest.
2. I enjoy my sense of humor and use it to have fun; I love being spontaneous; it is refreshing.
3. When I am authentic and express my true feelings, I am in my power.
4. When I am afraid, hurt, sad, or angry, I sit with the feeling, talk about it, journal; I have the courage to use my feelings for growth.
5. When I feel empty inside, I run to a friend, center myself, journal, take a walk; this takes courage.
6. Giving and receiving love is sufficient; I am truly free when I am being myself.

7. When I move outside my comfort zone, I look past the fear and toward the thrill and satisfaction of achieving my dreams.
8. I acknowledge and appreciate my accomplishments and talents.
9. I stay centered, mindful, focused, and conscious.
10. Because I know I am a powerful, spontaneous, courageous, and free woman, I accept and love myself and have no need for outside approval.

She is getting a good grip on the rewards to living this way. Nancy has done an excellent job of taking the risks each day that her new rules require of her. She is also noticing that there are still moments that she seeks her old rewards and has found she is at peace with that. She no longer flogs herself for wanting the comfort and safety that used to be so appealing. Her friend Lidia recently shared this e-mail exchange:

I talked to Nancy to discuss her amazing experiences lately as a facilitator that she shared in a recent email. She wrote that email and then sat on it for quite a while before she sent it. She said it felt weird and challenging to send something that sounded like she was bragging about herself. I think this is hugely important for all of us— the comfort level or lack thereof of owning our gifts. It also seems like a very central part of the process of transformation (getting out of the old mold that keeps stamping us into the same shape over and over). So yes! to Nancy for sharing even though it was uncomfortable and for challenging herself to expand her view of self. **Lidia**

My current class at the Court Clinic is doing very well. We are back on Step 1, so I have changed a few things for more interaction and participation from the class. I find that my attitude about this whole situation has changed. When I started, I described myself as working with a bunch of drug-addicted, alcoholic, crazy women.

(Anything to belittle my work and be safe in case I failed.) What I know I am doing is facilitating the opportunity for women to look at better ideas and ways of living a sober and fulfilling life. These women are not so different from any of us. They are just a little more lost. My wish is that they have learned as much from me as I am learning from them. They can be challenging at times, but then I guess I have been challenging at times too! We work hard in this class and we have fun. What a great combination. **Nancy**

Things to Remember:

1. **There is a hidden benefit for what we do.**

2. **The benefit rarely makes sense to us and doesn't seem worth the price we pay. We are more aware of the price we pay and how much we dislike paying it, than we are aware of the reward and how we are responsible for our behavior.**

8

Fear of the Light: Accepting Yourself As You Are

"Our deepest fear is not that we are inadequate. Our deepest fear is that we are powerful beyond measure. It is our light, not our darkness, that most frightens us. We ask ourselves, who am I to be brilliant, gorgeous, talented, and fabulous? Actually, who are you not to be? You are a child of God. Your playing small doesn't serve this world. There's nothing enlightened about shrinking so that other people won't feel insecure around you. We were born to make manifest the glory of God within us; it is not just in some of us—it's in everyone! And as we let our own light shine, we unconsciously give other people permission to do the same. As we are liberated from our own fear, our presence automatically liberates others!"

Marianne Williamson, *A Return to Love*

These words of Marianne Williamson ring true for many of us. They were powerful enough that Nelson Mandela used them in his inaugural speech when he became the president of South Africa. As stirring as these words are, it seems that few people are willing to accept the real greatness inside them.

I regularly meet people who wish for greatness, who wish they felt that way, but spend their lives fighting with their insecurities. They are so involved with what they fear or what's wrong that they don't have time to uncover what is most wonderful.

Indeed, it is the fear of being great that is the most difficult to overcome. I often see people struggle with themselves, wishing on the one hand that there is something awesome inside, and at the same time, fearing that what is inside is awful. The easiest way to deal with this dilemma is to compromise, to act as if we're pretty good, but not really great. On the surface, it appears as humility and can even carry a certain nobility.

Underneath, however, it feels like unworthiness. Time and again, I have encountered people who have finally come to grips with their feelings of unworthiness. They understand the roots, how it affects them, what it costs to live with that feeling, and on the verge of stepping out of it, they hit a barrier—the barrier of "what if."

A whole host of unknowns rise up that speaks to us of our fear of greatness. What would happen if I claimed my greatness? What if I'm not as great as I hope? What will happen to my relationships if I start showing up with more confidence? Will people think I'm arrogant? What if I claim my dream, and then have to live up to it? Do I have the strength to sustain it?

There exists a feeling in many of us that living with unfulfilled potential while knowing we could have been great is better than trying greatness and risking the fall. Actually failing at pursuing our dreams seems so much more painful than living with not trying. We can always find a reasonable excuse to explain why we didn't try. There is always the opportunity to blame it on something or someone outside our control. The following is a story that Kathy, the school principal, told me about her life.

I spent most of my life being too afraid to step up to the plate and ask for what I wanted. I felt I had some talents and skills, therefore people sometimes offered me things. This was pretty much the way I got ahead: waiting for the next "powerful someone" to notice I was worth having around. That led to a tendency to manipulate those outcomes that I wanted. (Because I knew I really wanted to do certain things, i.e., teach, be an administrator, etc., but it was not OK to risk putting myself out there.) Therefore, being noticed became a priority but it had to be in a way that didn't feel too risky. I didn't risk finding out that the other people DID notice me but found me wanting.

It led to a willingness to take what was offered, instead of going for what I really wanted. I feel that the first half of my life was lived by default, that I didn't so much make decisions about what I wanted to do as accept what others thought I should do.

For instance, when I was teaching at an elementary school, a principal from another building suggested that if I would become a counselor, he could give me a great job as half-time counselor, half-time gifted education teacher. I didn't much want to be a counselor, really, and was in the process of taking administration classes, but this was someone who should KNOW what I was good at, and I didn't want to disappoint him.

I hadn't yet learned to trust my own judgment, so why start now? It was safer to accept someone else's choice for me. I could feel valued and honored that he wanted me to do this. It was how I let myself feel special—wait for someone else to notice and reward me.

This also meant that, along the way, I held back from taking natural and desired steps out of the shadows of others. (i.e., remaining an assistant principal for several years rather than becoming a principal, etc.) I desperately wanted those "powerful someones" (most of whom looked like my dad to me!) to think I was the best, or the brightest, or their "favorite." And I would move forward when given enough encouragement. (In other words, I wanted them to ASK me to do it, rather than ask them for the opportunity). But stepping out and laying claim to who I am and what I need was way too risky.

I gained much strength from this behavior. I became very good at reading other people's feelings (watching for their approval before daring to voice something was a part of manipulating for their "reward"). I became a "do-er" ... a person who takes on every project and does it extremely well, in order to impress those "powerful someones" and make them look good. I was getting a reward of their gratitude and attention. I was able to do many things really well; it was important to me to be good at everything I tried (in order to get that approval and attention).

Conversely, I paid some prices. I didn't take charge of my own destiny until a couple of years ago. I never believed I could. I have been a chameleon, in order to fit in with whatever "powerful someone" was in charge at that time. I've sacrificed my integrity by agreeing with things I didn't agree with. I wanted to stay out of the front line. I grew to resent the people in charge who I felt controlled my destiny. (Until I "got" that they didn't!)

It was important for me to be this way in order to stay safe. I was truly feeling unworthy and afraid that others saw that, too. If I spoke up and said, "Here I am!" the feeling was that they might just say, "So?" And their agreement with my own sense of insignificance would be too deadly. It was much safer to allow my talents and skills to be noticed in roundabout ways, or get attention in other ways, than to speak up and claim it.

Kathy ultimately took the risk to reveal her own brightness. She decided that the "powerful someone" in her life could be herself. Today, she is a school principal instead of an assistant. She is also president of the non-profit board she was elected to, instead of being a committee member. She gained these positions after taking the risk of clearly presenting herself as a qualified candidate. She didn't wait any longer for someone to notice her; she didn't wait to be asked. She saw in herself the talent and the ability and she stepped into the light. She no longer felt the need to manipulate to get what she wanted.

Kathy has encountered that part of her that wanted to pretend weakness. She clearly saw it for what it was and took the risk to face it. It wasn't as if all her feelings of fear disappeared and then she felt the courage to act. Courage is what we do in the face of fear, not what we do without it. There is no courage without fear.

As painful as it was, there was protection in feeling not good enough, in not standing out. When she dropped the protective armor of feeling "less than," she had to ask for what she wanted the whole time while dealing with the fear of "*what if?*" What if I'm not good enough to handle the responsibilities, what will my peers think? Where will this lead and can I deal with it?

Kathy didn't "get fixed" and arrive all lit up. I have known and worked with her for several years and was a confidant of her during the struggle. At the point of taking a step into the light, you might want to remember there is no one step. It isn't an arrival so much as a departing point.

The journey for Kathy began with the understanding that she was not a victim. This insight is a foundation to build on when followed with a commitment to tell the unspoken truth. When she began to tell that truth, she discovered how she had been living and how constrained she was by her rules.

I find that I have elements of several of the "ways of being" that we have already identified, and, in writing this, I am going to try to gel my thinking about them.

My Need to be Special: this is probably my central one. The very word "special" has come up so often in my own personal growth work that I know it's a core value for me.

As the youngest child of four, I remember feeling that I had to somehow shine in order to get love and attention. There was my oldest sister who was special just for being the oldest (in my view), my second sister, who was our "tree-climber" and risk-taker and all the things I was too afraid to be, and my brother, next to me in age, who was the only boy and doted upon as such. As well, he was, and is, charming and giving (I didn't really want to see that about him at the time, as I was really jealous!), and all of the extended family gave him much attention.

I recall feeling "left out" a lot, even feeling very rejected because my parents had not named me after a relative, as they had all my siblings. It was an interesting moment for me when, in my thirties, I said something about that to my mother. She was astounded. Her perception was that she had FINALLY gotten to name one of her babies a name she wanted, instead of appeasing some family member! But in my growing up years, that felt like I was somehow lacking.

Combined with several "endearing" comments from my brother, along the lines of, "well, you know they didn't want you anyway, you were a mistake," I found reason to make a decision about myself (probably several decisions). One of them was that I was not inherently OK, that I had to be somehow "special" in other ways in order to be loved and accepted.

As you can see, Kathy was not yet ready to ask herself the question Marianne Williamson posed, "Who am I to be brilliant, gorgeous, talented, and fabulous?" Kathy was mired in feeling unworthy and stuck in living out the rules of trying to be special. No matter how hard she worked at it (and Kathy was a very hard worker indeed), she could never overcome her feeling of being unworthy solely by practicing worthy behavior. Take a look at how hard she tried to become worthy.

I had to laugh at all of my dad's jokes so that I would be his special one and he would like me best. I felt I needed to be cute and lovable (This was difficult as I didn't see myself as cute or lovable), and be smarter than all the others.

I had discovered that I was smart (I got attention from my parents when I learned to read and write quite early), and, at a fairly early age, was told my tested IQ level was quite high (which impressed my parents). I invested a great deal of myself in that knowledge and in being special through my intelligence. But again—conflict!

I soon discovered that peers were not as impressed by "smarties" and so I walked a fine line throughout school, in which I could be known as smart, get pretty good grades, but could not openly care about or work at it. At home and with adults, however, I needed to throw in that intelligent remark, that lofty vocabulary, that insight as if I knew more. And I did get attention for it.

I had to also be special in my peers' eyes, so I developed other ways of doing that. I made judgments about who was special enough for me to woo as a friend. People who were popular or powerful were the ones I wanted to be around, and I would be any kind of a chameleon in order to be accepted, and therefore be special by association. I had a kind heart, and cared about those whose feelings were hurt by some of these very popular folks, but my need to be special wouldn't allow me to find my friendships in less than the "in crowd."

There are several dimensions where I have discovered this theme of "Why can't I be special?":

1. It shows up a lot with my brother, who has gone on to accomplish great things and be revered for it. He is a strong and honest leader of integrity, a charming and humorous friend, and a man whom family, friends, and colleagues admire. And I continue to ache for the attention he gets for his accomplishments (especially from family members), even though I am so proud of him for them

(Tears here). "It feels very shallow and petty to admit that I continue to be jealous of the feelings others have for my brother, and to admit that I have had a wall between us for years because of my fears (that I don't measure up). I have never been able to be real and intimate with him because of this wall.

2. Even with my husband, who is starting more and more to shine his light on the world, I have twinges of that need to be special. He, more than anyone, understands it and helps me through those times, though. (Tears are definitely flowing.)

3. When in a class or seminar, I discovered that I didn't need to be the best (as I used to think I did), but rather I needed the professor, facilitator, or whatever "powerful someone" to THINK I was best, or like me best. I wanted to be the "special one."

4. In spiritual pursuits, I have often read that we are all one, that the divine power who created all shines equally in all of us. I believe that. But I hated hearing it the first few times. That meant I could NEVER be special, because special meant being different from and, yes, BETTER THAN OTHERS! So, arrogance was a part of my quest and colored many of my interactions with others, as well. (Remember my judgments about who was good enough to be friends with?)

5. When taking on a job or committee assignment, I find ways to outshine anything the "powerful someones" in charge could have expected. Thus, I am special and get attention for that. I feel accepted and validated when I stand out in those ways. I overdo and spend way too many hours doing, and commit to things that I don't need to do, in order to be special (do you see a lot of "do" references?) It certainly was never enough to just "be." This is also about being liked, but in my life, those two strings are tied very close together.

6. In my career, I found roles that offered me recognition and attention, but was afraid of the risk of stepping into full leadership, until lately. I always found ways to "stand out," like implementing new programs, etc., but pulled back from the risk of asking for the "top spot." You see, as much as I wanted that feeling of specialness, I had decided long ago that I really was NOT special. In subordinate positions, there was safety from exposure. I could do big things, special things, and get attention, without the risk that others would find out I really wasn't special at all.

7. In friendships: I keep them pretty surface and ask a lot of questions about the other person. It lets me look caring and loving and giving. All of those things are true, to some extent, but it's also about not giving away anything about me. I do much better at this now, and have been cutting this "string" assiduously. But I still have a tendency to keep friendships at a distance and not be real with them, to have a ton of friends but not deep friendships, to skate safely on the surface.

Kathy has done a very courageous job in taking off her mask and revealing the shadow self. She had hoped we wouldn't notice this part of her and that she could ignore it as well. I encourage you to know yourself in the same way, to know the elements of your mask and the truth that lies unspoken underneath. Kathy had avoided this because she felt more acceptable when she was ignorant of how she was behaving. When she opened up to the truth, she initially felt some guilt, remorse, and shame. Speaking the truth didn't feel like it was leading to acceptance, nor did it feel like the beginning of "letting her light shine" like Marianne Williamson had suggested. It felt like the opposite.

The path into self-acceptance is a bit counter-intuitive. There is a prevalent belief that, under our warts and blemishes there is perfection inside each of us. The usual expectation is that self-acceptance will entail letting go or working through our flaws and then being affirmed and convinced of our strengths. Kathy, like most of us, wanted to accept herself as she thought she "could be" and not as she was. She knew she needed to change and (quite logically) believed that if she wanted to feel better about herself she had to "become" a better person. And like Kathy, the assumption of most people is that they need to pare away the flaws. They also believe they worry too much about their weaknesses and that they should learn to focus almost solely on their strengths. If they could do this, they expect the feelings of "less than" will somehow disappear. The process is actually different from what you might expect.

Kathy clearly illustrates the start of this process. She believed she had never really been acceptable and had developed the intention of making herself "special" in the hope that she could then feel acceptable and worthy. She thought she had known the truth. The "truth" was that she wasn't acceptable and that she had to be something other than what she was in order to be loved and accepted. She was sure of that. If she could only agree with others, support others' ideas and plans, listen to others' problems, then she would be loved. When she began to understand that her behavior patterns were based on being a chameleon in order to be loved, she thought she had found "the answer."

Kathy thought that all she needed to do was become more assertive to solve the chameleon issue. She started by focusing on sharing her thoughts and feelings more freely. She would tell herself that the next time she had an idea that was unusual or provocative she would declare it. She also resolved to speak her mind about her feelings, especially those feelings that were likely to create conflict.

During those times when she had time to be reflective, she could clearly see how and where she should address this issue. She could recall situations and replay them in her mind while rehearsing her new correct answers. She could also predict the future events and people she would need to address in this new way. Unfortunately, when the moment came, she would mostly notice it only after it passed, or she would find some special exception for the occasion at hand. (If you have been in a similar position, you can probably relate; you can recognize her protestations of "I would have spoken up but the timing wasn't right," or "It wouldn't be fair to them; they had so much more on their minds." When we are afraid to change, there is always some excuse to avoid doing it in the moment we're in.)

Kathy found herself in a struggle with her own reluctance to speak up. She knew that she "should" speak out and be heard, and she also thought she would like herself more if she did. She knew that she was dealing with the issue of self-acceptance, and she had somehow figured that she would be acceptable when she conquered her chameleon nature and became more assertive. She also had settled on a strategy of working on the behavior where it showed up in her daily life. She believed that if she could only overcome those "bad habits," she would arrive at self-acceptance.

Like the man who was looking for his keys in the wrong place (under the street lamp) only because it was easier to see where there was more light, Kathy was looking for the key to her lack of acceptance where it broke the surface of her consciousness, not where it had begun. She recognized this need to avoid by being a chameleon, and so believed that this was the core issue. When she accepted the challenge of really knowing herself, she discovered that under the chameleon was a commitment to being seen as special and the belief that being special would ensure her acceptance by others.

That commitment was based on a decision she had made about herself. She had decided at a very young age that she wasn't acceptable as she was and needed to try to be special to gain acceptance. She believed that "powerful someones" (people like her father) would only find her loveable "if"...IF she performed to a high level, IF she supported and agreed with them, IF she made THEM look good, IF she hid who she really was and changed her beliefs, attitudes, and values to fit that powerful someone's criteria. Before she ever chose to do "chameleon" in her life, she had decided she was not OK. Kathy chose to hide her light and only shine where it was safe. She chose to be a backdrop for other people's lights, only allowing herself to glimmer a little here and there, always watching for the powerful someone's displeasure with that, in which case she would pull back.

A struggle that she experienced in dealing with these new "understandings" was that on the one hand, she had determined that she was not worthy and that she had to agree with everyone, blend in with them, support them. On the other hand, she believed she had to be more assertive. As you have probably guessed, the "blending in" won out more often than the assertive did. This new awareness initially caused even more conflict because she now felt bad about being unable to change this behavior!

Dealing with the part of her that chose to be a chameleon, however, was like pulling the top off a weed. It just grows back in a few days unless you get to the root. To move forward, she needed to accept herself as she was. This was her real starting point.

The challenge for Kathy was that she couldn't see past her own judgments. She really didn't think she was worth it. Kathy had fallen into a trap. She was stuck in a cycle that always leads her back to the beginning. It goes like this:

I don't feel worthy because I don't accept myself. I don't accept myself because I don't know myself. I don't know myself because I believe I should be someone different than who I am. I believe I should be someone different so I change myself into who I think others want me to be. The more I change to suit others the more I feel like a fraud. The more fraudulently I act, the less worthy I feel. (Back to the beginning)

Like a hamster on a wheel, no matter how fast she moved, she never made progress. She had learned that self-worth was an issue but she still didn't feel worthy. She thought she had to change to *become* worthy. She had to become more special, do more special things, and create a person of "specialness." She had, without realizing it, also included "being a person who spoke up all the time" as part of her picture of what a special person does. She saw all of what she considered to be her chameleon self to be flawed and didn't see that it was an integral part of her strength.

If she changed enough, she knew she would become lovable and would, earn, the self-worth that she needed. Therein lay the trap. This is the biggest obstacle to those who are on a path of personal development. *The trap is the notion that "I am changing to become better. If I change enough, I will become good enough. If I become good enough I can accept and love myself."*

It is a seductive pitfall on the path to change.

The Pitfall

"Learning to love oneself is the greatest love of all."

This is a dangerous obstacle on the path of self-discovery. It is almost impossible not to fall into this pitfall during the quest for self-knowledge. The question isn't whether you will step into it, but for how long you stay trapped. This is the trap. Each of us comes to this journey with a strong desire to change. This isn't a philosophical thinking about change but a gut-driven hunger for it. Without that hunger, few people would pay the price and spend the time; the work is just too hard.

That hunger is usually driven by the need inside to find peace with who we are. That peace only comes with self-acceptance. *Self-acceptance is thought of as the end product of change; that is, people think that when they have changed enough they will accept themselves.* Unfortunately, when your foundation is feeling unworthy, to change is to build a house on a weak foundation.

Building a beautiful house on a weak foundation doesn't change the foundation and make it stronger; it's the other way around. A weak foundation changes the beautiful house that it can't properly support. You may convince others who don't live in that structure that it is beautiful but those who live there live with the insecurity that the house will one day fall.

Kathy had been living in just such a house. She had come to recognize that she had spent her life trying to build worthiness on a deep sense of dislike for herself, and it hadn't worked. She started thinking she was a victim to her father's judgments. She then recognized the decision she had made, that she wasn't acceptable. She had arrived at the first critical choice, that she was not a victim. She then started to explore the truth that she had set up a way of being special and that her rules were what was driving her life. So far, so good. When faced with this truth, she didn't like what she saw. She had that gut-driven hunger to change. She started to struggle with her drive to be special just as she used to struggle with her need to be a chameleon. Her life became a battleground as she started to notice how often and in how many ways she buried her feelings behind a façade of making herself special.

Kathy was now wrestling with herself. She entered each new day squared off against an opponent that lived in her own skin.

Here is the problem. Imagine, if you would, two wrestlers facing each other (not the TV wrestlers but the Greco-Roman kind). The wrestlers are evenly matched in size and experience. Wrestling is a war that is fought close in. The wrestlers close in and grab each other and the struggle begins. They never take their eyes off each other and never ever turn their back on the opponent.

In wrestling, the match continues until one person pins the other or until the required time runs out. Then a victor is declared and it is finished. A struggle with yourself is different. The match is never over; you may be on top now but, as soon as your attention slips, so does your advantage. The match never ends; there is never a final victory, just a never-ending struggle. Think about the struggles going on within you. Maybe it's with exercise, being committed, shyness, or diet. Most often, these are see-saw affairs with a moment's success being followed by failure. First, you have the upper hand; then the opponent does.

So it goes in a struggle with one's self. You are fighting a piece of you. Your opponent knows what you know, is as strong as you are, and knows your secret strategy. How can you win a fight against you?

For those who have this secret struggle, there is hope. There is victory available but it is not the victory you thought you would have. My struggle was with shyness. I felt extremely confident in my thoughts and abilities in many situations, except social ones. I knew I was shy and didn't like it. I wrestled to overcome that shyness each time I entered a social setting.

The fight was always the same. I would find myself dreading each encounter, but also be steeling myself for the fight. I would swear that this time would be different; this time I would overcome the shyness. As the time grew nearer, I could feel the tension increase as I would grasp the shyness inside and try to wrestle it into submission. I knew the enemy and kept my focus on it, always in front of me.

When I would approach the door to a party, I remember being filled with apprehension instead of excitement. I would sometimes wonder if it was worth it. Should I just turn around and go, or should I just get a grip on myself and go on in?

After entering, I would feel the struggle intensify the closer I got to someone I wanted to meet. In keeping my shyness in front of me, it became all I could see or experience. It became my whole world. By the time I got close to talking to someone, I was so bound up in the struggle, I had no energy left to deal with the person in front of me. All that would come out when I began to speak was the incoherent stuttering and mumbles of someone overcome from the effort of fighting their personal demons.

The same was true for Kathy. She had been struggling with her desire to be more assertive. Sometimes she would feel she had won and stood up for her thoughts and ideas, and other times she would slip and feel like she had failed.

The following exercise is one that helped her create clarity around this issue. Most of us who begin a path of growth have a secret "hit" list of traits we would like to rid ourselves of. This is part of the underlying trap in the growth business. We also have, over the years, noticed the good qualities that we would rather not change.

Kathy's list looked something like this:

Things I thought were "good" traits (that I wanted to keep) about my self:	Things I did not like about myself (wanted to change in order to be "better"):
+	−
1) Outgoing 2) Friendly 3) Cheerful 4) Smart 5) Loving/nurturing 6) Do-er	1) Dishonest (would hide things from others even by lying so they would not see me as imperfect) 2) Cowardly (physically afraid of taking risks, and also afraid to speak up and say what I thought) 3) Chameleon (related to #2) 4) Unattractive (thought my appearance was what could help me be loved and accepted) 5) Disorganized

Kathy would try to amplify those traits on the left side of the page while minimizing those on the right. She would have spent her days, if she could, only exercising those qualities that she liked. She was involved in personal growth to try to "exorcize" those traits that she didn't approve of. "Well what's wrong with that?" you may ask. I can't tell you how many times I have heard that response. Why shouldn't we do that? Why would anyone want to encourage behavior in themselves that they did not approve of?

Think back for a moment to Kathy's quote at the beginning of the first chapter. *"There was always a feeling of something missing, or something out of place. It was as if the picture of my life that looked so complete, upon closer inspection would prove to have little unfinished gaps, places where the paint didn't quite match or the colors on top were just covering up uglier colors underneath. There seemed to be more that I wanted in life. I was always proving myself, but feeling like a fraud."*

That feeling of being a fraud is "what's wrong with that." Each of us have parts we like and admire as well as those we don't like and wish we were rid of. To try to kill off those traits is like trying to kill a part of yourself. To not explore and accept those parts will leave you feeling like a fraud, as if there is paint covering up something ugly underneath.

The saddest part of this is that what is underneath isn't inherently ugly. Only our lack of acceptance makes it seem so. Kathy was full of judgment about feeling like a chameleon, just as I was full of judgment about being shy. We had no doubt that the problem lay in having those traits. The only solution to having them was to rid ourselves of them. It seems almost impossible to make the leap to the understanding that our judgment was the problem, not our traits.

Over the last 30 years, I can't count the times I have heard the importance of self love. I have heard it in songs, stories, books, and seminars. I have heard it in church, on TV, and as advice from strangers. It always seems the same, I won't be truly happy without love, and I won't be able to love others until I love myself.

As trite as the sayings have become, they reflect a deep and abiding truth. I woke up to the fact that I was a hollow, distant, and aloof man in 1973. It was clear to me that I didn't love myself even though I liked much of who I was. I set out on a mission to learn who I was and to learn self love. Like the knights in search of the Holy Grail, I was dedicated to do whatever it took for as long as it took. The first challenge on the journey was a rude awakening. There were countless people telling me to love myself and none who seemed able to tell me how.

I thought that if I looked long enough and was sincere enough that the right teacher would come along. I had read somewhere that when the student is ready the teacher appears. I thought that meant that if I made myself available with an earnest desire that a teacher would show up. I thought it was a test of my patience—that my waiting patiently showed my readiness to learn. I ultimately found that it wasn't a test of time; rather, it was a test of my being someone who was capable of learning. I wanted teaching but wasn't capable of being taught. I was so full of judgment there was no room left inside for understanding. I had to clear the judgment out of the way before I would be capable of learning something new. It wouldn't matter if I patiently waited until hell froze over, I had to empty myself of what I was full of before I could refill with something new.

Kathy, too, was full of judgment. She had heard her entire life about the importance of assertiveness. There were books written about it and seminars to attend to enhance it. Everyone knew it to be the right way to be. She accepted the "fact" that how she acted was a problem. It seemed inconceivable to her that she could ever accept being a chameleon and impossible that there was a benefit to it. She, too, was filled with judgment.

An amazing thing started to happen to Kathy when she stopped trying so hard to change what she judged and started to accept it. She started to notice the strengths and abilities that had lain hidden beneath her judgment and had been honed through her life.

I have gained much strength from my "way of being." I do read people's emotions and spoken/unspoken language rather easily. I sense others' feelings and thoughts. In working with colleagues, I'm able to help work through tense situations or find diplomatic solutions because of this.

In my relationship with my husband, my need to be a "do-er" meshes well with his needs, most of the time. (I can go too far with that!) I have accomplished a lot and gained a lot of respect for my work and my ability.

I have done a lot for other people, taking on tasks and responsibilities that were too much for them or that needed doing, thus making myself indispensable (and special!), but also truly filling a need for someone else.

I have developed an ability to see things from other people's viewpoints. When I overdo that, it becomes wishy-washy and indecisive. But when I utilize it well, it's strength.

I have discovered why being this way is important to me. My father's love was vital to me and I felt at an early age that I would only get that if I were somehow much more special than I had decided I really was. I had to "do" more, shine more (but in safe ways), in order to be loved and accepted. He had not finished college due to WWII, and always felt somehow "less than" because of it. (Both of his sisters did finish and were teachers.) Therefore, he placed an even higher premium on his own native intelligence and on his vocabulary and on ours.

Each of the traits that made up a chameleon was beneficial some of the time. The first trait, to read others' reactions before having one herself, relied on her innate people-reading skills. She had also honed those skills to a razor's edge through constant practice. She had become adept at understanding what people wanted, as well as often understanding what they wanted and couldn't always express. Adding this insight to her holding back her opinions (until she knew she was right or that she had an unusual or insightful viewpoint) had created a reputation for her of being a sharp and insightful team member. It created many opportunities to work on the projects and in the groups she admired most.

That she focused on what she did, found ways to shine, and sought to do impressive work helped her develop job skills that were to become indispensable when she decided she was ready to step up from assistant principal to principal.

In fact, each of the traits that made up the chameleon was taken from the gifts that she was born with. She had developed them through overuse and may have applied them in ways that were counterproductive, but they had become very important resources.

Each person who travels the road to self acceptance finds the same embarrassing truth—that they have tried to kill off the source of their greatest gifts. I found, after accepting my shyness, that one of the underlying traits of being shy was a feeling of being a separate observer of life, watchful and aware. It was later that I noticed that this was the basis of my objectivity and insightfulness, two of the most important and defining traits in my character and my career.

As Kathy found the value hidden in the chameleon, she felt her judgments ease a little. As her judgments eased, she felt less like struggling to overcome that part. With the end of the struggle, she no longer viewed that part of her as an adversary that had to be watched constantly. In time, she felt comfortable not watching it at all. It no longer absorbed her whole focus; it no longer looked like her whole self.

One day, without really knowing when, she found herself feeling at ease with herself. The part she had been fighting, although still a part of her, had changed from a struggle to a source of pride. Much like a book that she was reading, while in her lap has her whole attention to the exclusion of all the other books available, her chameleon had her attention to the exclusion of all the other traits she had available. Eventually, she placed that book back on the shelf. When that happened, she could again notice the other volumes on the shelves. In that same way, she was now free to explore the parts of herself that had gone unnoticed while she had been so absorbed.

One of the characteristics she found was the ability to be assertive. It was scary at first. She was trying out new behavior and needed a little practice. Eventually she found it fit nicely with the skills she developed during her earlier years as a chameleon. As for what became of the chameleon? She still has days where she sits back and thinks instead of speaking up, and there are still times she gives up what she wants in order to please others. The difference is in how she treats herself when these times occur. She no longer uses them to prove her lack of worth. She no longer struggles trying to kill them off. She had finally escaped the pitfall of changing herself in order to feel acceptable.

She had discovered the most important change on the path. If you recall the split page with her positive and negative traits, she had been trying to eliminate those on the right side of the page. She thought that was the important change for self-acceptance. As it turns out, the most crucial change for self-acceptance is to erase the positive and negative signs on the top of the page. Take the line down that divides the halves and let the parts that you try to hide come out of the shadow and into the light.

Kathy has had an encounter with her fear of her own greatness and finally decided that she could shine. She has finally had the courage to disagree with the belief she had carried all those years that she was only special when she was told so by others. She has begun a journey full of twists and turns that will draw her into a life beyond her imagining. Usually the only guarantee is that it won't be boring.

Things to Remember

1. **False humility is still false.**

2. **It often feels easier to deal with the pain of mediocrity than the fear of greatness**

3. **One way to avoid greatness is to become obsessed with what's wrong.**

4. **You have to act in the face of fear, not wait for the absence of fear.**

5. **You can never win a struggle with yourself.**

6. **The path to acceptance leads through integrating the traits you don't like, not by eliminating them.**

THE FOURTH CHOICE OF FREEDOM

9

Change Your World

"No man is an island entire of itself, every man is a piece of the continent, a part of the main."

John Donne

When we start to change, each of us seems more aware of our separate and isolated sense of self than we are of the interconnectedness with our families and society. We have noticed how others have contributed to the way we are and may even have felt they were entirely responsible. Somehow, when it comes to change, most of us end up believing we have to do it by ourselves, alone.

This makes the change process more difficult. It is obvious that, without the council and input of others it is very difficult to see ourselves and even harder to continue during the tough time without their support.

What seems less obvious to many people is the ongoing role that our family and friends play in keeping us the way we have been. It is very obvious to parents how friends, TV, movies, school, and social trends affect their children. Those same parents seem to believe that they are immune to such influences themselves.

The culture that exists in your workplace is as powerful an influence as is school for a child. Each business has its own set of values; and it rewards employees who work within those values. Those who don't are either pressed until they fit in or they pay the price of being held back or let go.

The support of your friends is also very important, just as it was as a teen. You picked your friends because they liked you and were comfortable with how you lived. Each time you change, that comfort level changes also. They will do what they can to bring you back to a life that was comfortable for you both.

If you think back to your rules for living, it is easy to believe that those rules applied to our lives only, but that isn't entirely true. When Nancy agreed to be nice it wasn't only about her, it became an unspoken agreement with her friends and family, as well as her co-workers. You could always expect her to be nice no matter what. When she started to break that rule, those who knew her felt that she was breaking an agreement with them. Even though they had never spoken about it, Nancy's consistent habits and patterns of behavior were taken as a promise of how she would act in the future. Those who knew her felt betrayed when she was more assertive than nice.

Imagine what happened to Michael, who took the easy way out, when he started to face up to the difficult choices and decisions in life. He was a gregarious and outgoing person who was a natural leader.- He has a great sense of humor and love of beer. People are drawn to him. He was adept at seeing the faults of bosses, companies, policies, and bureaucracies, and making fun of their flaws.

When he decided that he could do something to change things, he knew he had to stop drinking and accept the responsibilities that come with leadership. His friends felt that he was making a mistake and was abandoning them. They missed the old Mike who was so much fun and so irresponsible. They tried to get him to come back in the fold, have another drink and be one of the guys. Each one of his friends was exerting pressure by trying to reestablish the bonds of their friendship.

Those bonds of friendship are like the strings that tied down Gulliver. Each of those rules Mike lived by was like a string tied to every person he knew. A string that kept him bound to his old way of behavior. Each time he tried to change, his companions would try to pull him back into line using the bond of their friendship. His friends, like Nancy's, thought his habitual behaviors were an agreement. If Mike tried to move away from his normal behavior, they would pull him back because in their minds he had agreed to be that way.

Each person around you is exerting social pressure on you to stay the same—those who want you to change only want you to change in ways that are convenient to them. This is not a conspiracy against you but one that you are actively involved with. You chose your friends and have trained your family and co-workers to support your way of being. Nancy had built a world that supported and demanded that she be nice, just as Mike had about taking the easy way out. We think of ourselves as an island. We feel our isolation and the distance between us and miss the enormity of the impact that others exert upon us each day.

In this way we have, without noticing it, created a mold for our lives. This mold is driven by that subtle and continuous pressure. It acts as the form we press ourselves into each day to make sure that we maintain the same shape as the day before.

Just as an automobile plant has giant hydraulic presses that create identical shapes from metal, your world has been set up to create a shape for you. Imagine for a moment that you are in the Ford plant and in front of you is one of those presses. There are two critical parts to this operation—the machine that supplies the force and the mold that determines the shape. Each few seconds an identical sheet of metal slides under the press and the enormous force of the press stamps it into the specific shape of the mold. Each piece, created by tremendous pressure, is identical to the last piece. Each piece is a Ford, and even if you decided that you would rather have a Mercedes, you would continue to get Fords as long as the mold stays unchanged.

Such is your life. The mold is created by your rules for living and the habitual way you live them out. Many of these no doubt came to light when you noticed your way of being and the rules for living that went with it. In effect, it is the sum of your "shoulds." The pressure is created through the ties that you have to other people. It is measured not only by the social pressure to perform in ways that are consistent with their expectations, but also by the force of your intention to be seen a certain way.

Why is this important? This is a barrier to the success of many people who have mastered the first three steps but resist the fourth. In thinking of yourself as essentially separate, you may think that changing your life is limited to changing the way *you* think and act. If you are successful at that and go back to your world as it was, that world will begin stamping you back to your original shape. Each day it will attempt to force you to revert to how you were. You may have the strength to resist at first, but ultimately you will find yourself worn down by the unrelenting pressure.

Our lives are littered with examples of this. If you decide to give up cigarettes, your smoking friends will tease you to start again; if you give up drinking, they may offer you a drink. When you go on a diet, you will be offered sweets, "Go ahead—one won't hurt," or "You can start your diet tomorrow." We have all felt the pressure to return to what is comforting to others.

One example I have often seen in this work is when a person is working to let go of using anger to control a spouse. This was the case with a friend I'll call Joe. When Joe told his wife Mary what he was trying, her response was a skeptical "We'll see." Joe was actually doing fairly well with this—but Mary responded with a series of small antagonisms that ultimately led Joe back to anger. Whenever he slipped, Mary would be quick to state that she *knew* he couldn't do it. Eventually, Joe gave up and they comfortably fell back into the pattern that *Mary* had originally wished would change; she was the one who had pushed him to try the new behavior in the first place!

In time, you will convince some people to support and even encourage the new direction you have chosen. Others may never find in themselves the generosity and courage to embrace what they don't understand. If you have come this far, it is imperative that you take this next step. Oddly, as much as people resist change in their own behavior, they seem to resist changing their environment even more.

To change yourself you *must* change your environment. This means that you will have to set boundaries with those people and situations that cannot or will not let go of your past. More importantly, it means that you must find people and situations that will support you in your quest. Your world needs to become an ally—not an adversary to your work. As with freedom, changing your world requires some hard choices, which I identify as steps. The rest of the chapter is devoted to these steps.

Step 1: Tell the Truth

The first step may be the hardest: tell the truth about how you have really been. Telling the truth means more than not telling lies. It means opening up parts of yourself that have been hidden.

Most people will admit what they know about the life they have lived. They will share their thoughts about themselves when they feel safe. This isn't good enough. You have to unmask. It may be a struggle at first; it may even feel embarrassing or shameful.

When I first wrote about feeling special, I was acutely embarrassed. I thought I had revealed too much, that I would lose the respect of people who knew me. Oddly enough, those who knew me best didn't find this revealing at all. They thought it was about time that I woke up and realized how I had been acting. The only real difference is that now we *all* are clear on how I pretend to be. This makes it much harder to get away with the pretense.

One of the first challenges in being honest is how to reveal what you aren't yet conscious of yourself. The key lies in the perceptions of others. You have to look in *that* mirror. Find someone who is trustworthy, honest, insightful, and truly has your best interests at heart. Use their perceptions as a mirror. Ask them what they see in you. What do they think your consistent rules for living might be? Do they have an idea about what your underlying intention is?

When I started to open, I was nervous about asking others; I was afraid of what I might hear. Besides, maybe they hadn't noticed any odd behaviors. Maybe they thought I wasn't like that at all. I was worried if I brought it up, they would now see who I was. I wouldn't take the risk of their rejection.

I think I was only able to take this risk when I trusted myself enough to handle the consequences. I had to be willing to live exposed, vulnerable, and in the light. When you trust yourself this much you can take the risk to let people see you beneath the mask. That trust is a result of self-knowledge and acceptance. Without that, I was always afraid that others would see some unacceptable hidden part of me. I thought that if they did I would then get blindsided by their judgment and rejection. As I have faced up to myself, I have begun to trust myself to be OK, even in the midst of the disapproval of others.

To begin this process for yourself, find the "way of being" that fits you best. Don't get stuck on my lists. People are constantly telling me of new ones. Recently I had someone tell me he was sort of like "*I Want to be Liked*" —yet it wasn't quite right. When he shifted it to "*I Don't Want to Offend People,*" it felt just right. Sometimes a simple variation in the language can work wonders. You may find that the first "way" covers part of how you operate and two or three together explains much more.

When you have found a fit, spend time with a journal. Write about the "way of being" and how it has affected your life. What kind of impact has it had on your relationships? Has it affected your choice of friends or spouse? What are the consequences at work?

Spend the time writing to examine as many relationships as you can. While doing this journal, start a list of your "rules to live by." See how many you can discover. Notice the specific ways the rules have altered your life. When you do arrive at an example, write the example down in great detail. Don't be vague—be as specific as you can. Each of those rules ties you down. Each person with whom you use those rules is an unwitting accomplice in holding you back.

Find out what the secret rewards are for living this way. We do things to achieve rewards. What are yours? Remember Tom who was living out "*I'm not Worthy.*" He said:

I guess it was more important for me to protect myself from criticism than to take a chance. As long as I "did good" and kept a low profile, even though I didn't get praise, I didn't get criticized either. At least that way I could maintain a sort of secret self-esteem. Interestingly, as I think about, I still feel myself tense up whenever I think somebody is going to criticize me, and I have a really hard time accepting praise.

These benefits are almost always hidden. Tom's reward for keeping a low profile was avoiding criticism. This allowed him the benefit of finding his secret self-esteem. Tom had been able to justify his low profile for years. He would be occasionally challenged to change, but had managed to avoid the challenge. It wasn't readily apparent to him that he had a secret purpose in holding back, but it became clear with reflection.

The justifications are what we know. You may believe you have to be this way. Maybe you think Mom, Dad, society, or your history makes you behave this way. Perhaps, like many, you have made your excuses sound like nobility. You may believe you hold back for the benefit of others or out of politeness. This may sound good, and it may be partially true. All too often, it is a disguise for what you may be secretly getting from your behavior.

You will also find the genuine benefits that have come from your actions. These behaviors aren't crimes or sins—merely crutches. They are an overuse of an asset, in place of developing other abilities. Using them in this way has strengthened you and developed skills and abilities that you can capitalize on. Take time to appreciate the good things that have resulted from your actions.

Just as you are rewarded for your behaviors, you also pay a price. What has it cost you to be this way? What has the effect been on your relationships, your career, or your self-esteem? Steve summed up the price he paid in "I'm Smarter than you" like this:

I felt like Spock—a logical person but not a whole man. It wasn't clear to me for a long time that I hid in my thoughts. Thinking was familiar and safe; it was an easy place to hide. It cost me the warmth and joy that can only come from the heart. I found myself mostly feeling cool, aloof, and distant.

Understand that changing behavior will have a price also. Doing things differently will change the price you pay; it won't free you from paying prices.

Keep a daily journal on your progress. Write daily about your successes and failures. Don't expect instant total success; it may take a while to undo a deeply ingrained trait.

Things to Remember About the Truth:

1. **The truth means to unmask, not merely "don't tell lies."**

2. **Reveal your hidden intentions, with both the price and reward.**

3. **Keep a journal to record the journey to deeper levels of yourself.**

Step 2: Practice Self-Acceptance

The firm foundation for this work is self-acceptance. Any structure without a good foundation, no matter how well built, is bound to fail. The same is true with this. No matter how carefully you apply the lessons in this book, if you don't accept yourself it will be for naught.

Take a few minutes to review the split page exercise from Chapter 8. Do you really accept the parts of yourself that you have judged? Even when I thought I had embraced those aspects of myself, I found in my first stab at this that I was doing it from a desire to change them. In other words, I hadn't really accepted them at all. I had hidden my rejection behind a façade of acceptance. I have found no limit to my ability to trick myself.

After you have completed the exercise, take the risk to share the right hand column with a person you trust. Remember that secrets have power. The more you let out the secrets the less power they will have over you.

Your ability to share aspects of your "shadow" is an indication that you are starting to trust yourself enough to handle the consequences. This is an excellent sign that you are accepting yourself also. It is very difficult to share the parts of us that we don't love. The fear is that others won't love or accept us if they know these things. Usually the opposite will occur if you pick someone who has your best interests at heart. If they are objective, you will often find the opposite of what you fear will happen. People who share intimate details grow closer. This is not an exercise that should be carried to extremes. Nothing is as off-putting as someone who has become obsessed with themselves. Don't overburden your friends with a constant stream of revelation every time you see them. Pick someone carefully and share yourself occasionally in this way. Notice their reaction; if they seem truly interested, continue while there is interest. If they seem uncomfortable or dismissive, find someone who is more responsive.

"If it's worth doing it's worth doing poorly."

When I first heard these words, I thought the speaker had made a mistake. I was raised with "If it's worth doing, it's worth doing well." A few years ago, I heard someone say it differently and I finally realized how much sense this version made. I had to be willing to make mistakes, to do things poorly, in order to learn. I not only had to make mistakes; I had to accept that it was OK and a natural part of learning.

An important part of acceptance is an allowance to make mistakes. When I learned to juggle, the first instruction was to drop the balls, then do it again and again until I was comfortable dropping them. This may seem strange (it did to me at first) when the objective is to keep them in the air! In order to learn to get them to stay in the air I dropped them hundreds of times. It was an excellent idea to become comfortable with making mistakes early on. I didn't need the pressure of perfection or the self-judgment that goes with it.

As you work to change these behaviors, you will find many

occasions that you retreat to the actions that you were trying to leave behind. Expect it to be this way. Just like learning to drop the balls and being OK with that, you have to learn to drop the balls with this.

When you feel you have dropped the ball, don't hide it. There is, for many of us, an underlying sense of shame that goes with failure. Shame is what drives us to keep our secrets. Share your successes and your failures. Sharing your perceived failure will help you avoid hiding yourself from fear or shame.

Things to Remember About Self-Acceptance:

1. Self-acceptance is the foundation of change.

2. Embrace failures; don't be ashamed if you don't succeed at first.

3. Share your successes and failures.

Step 3: Clarify Intention

One of the greatest challenges of my life has been to access the power of intention. When I first heard stories about amazing accomplishments by ordinary people, I was intrigued. I heard of mothers lifting cars off their children, or people being rescued from danger in disaster or war. When I encountered the same thing on a mountain in the Arizona desert, I wanted to know more.

Why does it require such drastic circumstances? Is there a way to achieve those results without the fear of death or loss? I discovered that there is a way, but it requires first of all an extraordinary effort of will and, secondly, enough faith in oneself to risk surrendering.

The ability to call on this force of will relies on your capability to focus. You must give up the convenience of confusion about who you are, what you are capable of, and especially, what you want. You have to get very clear about what your intention is and why. The reason that life-and-death situations reveal this to us is because in those moments all other desires go out the window and we focus deeply on one: *I want to live.*

Each day, you are presented with hundreds of choices and opportunities. You may find yourself desiring many things without really being focused on any one thing. For a while, you may be wishing for more money. That wish drifts into the desire for a happier marriage, which goes to wanting more respect at work, and so on. The solution to respect at work may require you to be more assertive, but this conflicts with your need to not make waves. This is important so that you can fulfill your intention to be likeable. In any moment, you may be clear on what you are thinking you want, but there is a simultaneous babble of internal voices crying out for other unmet needs. You need to quiet the voices inside. You must face up to what your underlying intention has been and satisfy it. Without this crucial awareness, each time you attempt to focus on what you *think* you want, you will be sabotaged by your deeper intention.

The second ability—to surrender—is based on self-trust. This means that you give up conscious control and let a deeper part of you take over. This is very different from quitting, and also very different from giving control to someone else. Those are acts based on lack of faith in oneself.

Surrender means allowing yourself to take risks by doing things that are outside your comfort zone. Essentially this forces you to act without knowing the outcome. Think back to the earlier quote by Gandhi: "Man is the center of a circle described by his own self-limiting beliefs." To surrender means you will now be intentionally operating outside that circle.

Surrender also means that you will be relying on your deep

inner strengths as well as the power of your unconscious mind. This is uncomfortable in that, until you try, you can't really be sure that you are strong deep inside, or that your inner mind is all that powerful. You probably haven't tried because you haven't been forced to do so. You have figured out how to cope with your normal world using the ordinary mental tools. This works quite well as long as you operate in familiar territory. But what about when you go outside the familiar, outside the known?

You may never wish to find out. I remember someone describing it like a map they had seen. This particular map had been drawn several hundred years ago at a time when the nature of the physical world was a mystery. The map was neatly drawn to the edge of the known world. At the boundary of the known world, the mapmaker had included some fierce looking dragons and the words, "There be dragons here."

All of us have such a map inside. It is an internal blueprint that tells us where we are safe and knowledgeable enough to comfortably operate. The more we trust ourselves and are willing to take risks, the larger the area included in that map. This map is the layout of your comfort zone. The dragons seem very real in the sense that, once you stray from the known, there are situations and challenges that will require you to operate in some unique and different ways.

Some of those situations may require you to abandon your normal control of your limits and call upon what's truly best in you. You won't know what that is until you take the risk to do it. In stepping outside your boundaries you may find that your dragons are like Lisa's pack of wild dogs; you may find that your known talents and abilities are more than ample to take care of what you had feared. Other times, you will find that your dragons truly are dragons and that your normal style just won't do this time. You will have to reach inside for something more. You will have to surrender who you think you are and what your limits *were* (even just a second ago!) to overcome the challenge in front of you.

I have encountered many people who have arrived at a place where they want to change. The life they have been living is no longer enjoyable. They say they want to change more than anything. The change they want, though, still eludes them. Usually I find the obstacle in their unwillingness to look deep inside and know themselves, or in a lack of trust in themselves. Intention isn't a wish or a want; it's a feeling of "I can't live without." Until you want it that bad, things won't change. What you want has to be that important. If it isn't, you probably won't make it through the barrier that separates intending from wishing.

Also check to make sure that what you are asking for is really what you want. I meet people who want to change to gain approval from others. They have the idea that if they become thinner, or more open, others will like them better. This is a flimsy premise upon which to base a life. Many people have found that no one likes them any better thin than thick, that what was really holding people away was how they acted because they didn't like themselves.

When you are clear that you are committed to a path that is your own, write it down. Think of it as a contract with yourself. Write out a detailed description of how your life would be different. Think about and plan for the changes that will be required in the situations in which you will find yourself. Don't leave it to chance that you will change your habits without a great deal of preparation and forethought. Write down the new list of rules that you will live by. Post them in a conspicuous place. Think about with whom they apply. Spend time visualizing encounters that you think will be challenging before you reach them.

Be as well prepared as you can. Nancy ("I want to be comfortable") has written hers to remind her where she is coming from and the direction of her future.

I Want To Be Comfortable and Safe
     1. Always be nice.
     2. Be cute and funny.

3. When I am afraid, hurt, sad, or feel threatened, I run to my safety net—food.
4. When I feel that utter emptiness inside myself, I run to my safety net—food.
5. Food = safety, acceptance and love, so I share, make food ,and give it as gifts to show love and receive love and acceptance.
6. Don't push yourself too far out of your comfort zone; it's scary out there.
7. I am not good enough, talented enough, smart enough, etc., and never will be; accept unworthiness.
8. When I am emotional, I go unconscious and eat, forgetting all other promises and commitments I have made.
9. Always find fault with my progress.
10. The only way to feel worthy, successful, talented, etc., is to get approval from others.

That is where she started; the following is how she currently lives:

I Am a Powerful, Spontaneous, Courageous, and Free Woman
1. Be honest.
2. I enjoy my sense of humor and use it to have fun; I love being spontaneous; it is refreshing.
3. When I am authentic and express my true feelings, I am in my power.
4. When I am afraid, hurt, sad, angry, I sit with the feeling, talk about it, journal; I have the courage to use my feelings for growth.
5. When I feel empty inside, I run to a friend, center myself, journal, take a walk; this takes courage.
6. Giving and receiving love is sufficient; I am truly free when I am being myself.
7. When I move outside my comfort zone, I look past the fear and toward the thrill and satisfaction of achieving my dreams.
8. I acknowledge and appreciate my accomplishments and talents.
9. I stay centered, mindful, focused, and conscious.
10. Because I know I am a powerful, spontaneous, courageous, and free woman, I accept and love myself and have no need for outside approval.

The last part of clarifying intention is to simplify the process. Life is complex; we all have more than enough to do. Each day is filled with projects and commitments. There is constant busyness and the frustration that comes with keeping up with deadlines.

These can all serve as distractions to important changes. I mentioned earlier how good I am at tricking myself; one of the ways I trick myself is to be too busy doing important things. When I have a change that is hard or frightening to make, I often become very involved with other projects until I forget what I was going to do.

If there is an important change in your future, clear your plate of some of the potential distractions. Start with an examination of those things you do out of a compulsion to be your old "way of being." See if you can revisit those agreements that you made to support the rules you live by.

Maybe you can't say "no," or you try to be super-person, or gain value by how much you do more than by who you are. Change the agreements that you made in support of how you have been. For most of us, this alone will clear our plates enough to stay present with the change we need to make.

Things to Remember About Clarifying Your Intention:

1 Intention is a deep force of will.

2 A new intention is only set in place where there is self-trust and self-acceptance.

3 The new intention needs to come from an authentic place in you.

4 Clearing up distraction will assist in a successful completion.

Step 4: Hunt Your Self Down

This is where things get fun and a little scary. It's time to track down the traits in yourself you want. Most people assume that what they are seeking is outside themselves. They think that if they are timid, they need to gain confidence, or if they are too task-oriented, they need to learn people skills, etc. They believe these traits don't exist in them but need to be added, like putting on a new set of clothes, or adding an option to their car.

We are full of surprises. Each of us has a host of unexpressed talents and abilities. These talents are waiting to be unblocked; they can only be expressed when we free ourselves from the barriers that come from our "ways of being." Like Gulliver in Chapter 5, we need to be free from the strings that have tied us to the past. With that freedom, you will find previously unseen abilities ready for you to develop and explore.

As I mentioned earlier, when I stopped struggling with shyness. I found the roots of being outgoing. I never would have found it while staying caught up in shyness. Many people are so obsessed in finding out all they can about what's *wrong* with them and whose fault it is that they can't see the greatness they have hidden inside.

The purpose of hunting yourself down is to find a way to release traits that have been hidden from view. Start with your new list of "Rules to Live By." Pick one that will require you to act very differently than you have in the past.

Choose a specific person or situation that applies to this trait. For instance, suppose one of your rules is that you don't create waves. You regularly find you compromise what you want to let others have their way. You know this is how you behave but are confused about how to change it. What you have found in yourself is compromise. What we will hunt down is the courage to speak up. Just as a hunter searches for the footprints of the beast they are hunting and follows them until they lead to the goal, you must follow the footprints that lead to your change.

Pick one person you have done this with recently. Set up an appointment with the express intention of dealing with this issue. Notice how you are feeling just thinking about this. Are you feeling nervous? Hands a little sweaty? GOOD. Hunters must know the footprints of the beast they are seeking. The footprint of the courage to speak up is fear. (Remember courage can't exist without fear.) In order to hunt down a part of you that is courageous, you must follow the "tracks" of fear. Most people who arrive at this spot stop. They want to wait until the fear subsides, telling themselves that *then* they will move on. Unfortunately, the fear won't subside until they have sufficient experience facing up to it. Don't stop and wait, you must follow the path that leads through your fear.

As you call the person to set up your appointment, the fear rises. This is how you know you are closer to the beast. When the appointed time comes, the fear is now seriously elevated. A part of you is whispering, "Don't do it!" You think you don't need to. You think of excuses to back out! You think of important projects that need your attention!! With each step closer to that rendezvous your fear increases. Those are the footprints that lead you to courage.

If you are lucky, you will have one of those magic moments. If the issue is big enough—Things To Remember About Clarifying Your Intention—you know that "one" you've been avoiding for years—you may find that in the moment of truth that your mind shuts down. All your carefully prepared dialogue goes out the window and the truth comes out. Something inside that has lain dormant comes to the surface—the need to be genuine and unmasked. This is a moment of power.

Don't panic. You may find yourself saying things that have been pent up for years. You may find that there are scores of issues that have been waiting for you to deal with. This is your opportunity to take the relationship to a new level, one of authenticity.

Your partner may be surprised by the seeming suddenness and

boldness of your statements. It may take a considerable amount of time to resolve the issues. You may find this is an appropriate time to seek outside support to help in the effort.

I suggest you start with manageable pieces. Save the meatier ones for when you have more experience. The following story by Crissy illustrates this well:

I knew I wanted to have more relaxation and ease in my life, but I often felt rushed and harried. Eighteen years ago, I found myself racing along the interstate to deliver the cupcakes for my daughter's preschool party with as much flurry and stress as if I were speeding a financial report to the board of a Fortune 500 company. It occurred to me then that I must be producing much of the stress in my life.

Life Success Seminars (www.LifeSuccessSeminars.com) has been responsible for so much has improvement in my life, but I still struggle with being relaxed. (I know my friends and family will raise their eyebrows at that because I can certainly put my feet up and have a good time.) I guess a better way to put it is that sometimes when I work, I have a rushed, "put-upon" sensation.

My "way of being" that creates that feeling is "I need to work as hard or harder than those around me." I came up with this as a child to avoid my mother's anger while she was working. Some of the rules that support this way of being were eye-opening to me:

1. *It's safer to resent others than be resented by them.*
2. *Add more work to any activity to justify feeling burdened.*
3. *If someone else is working and stressed—DANGER—offer to help.*
4. *While doing one task, think about all the tasks I want to do that day.*
5. *It's OK to keep those around me less competent so I can feel more competent.*
6. *When making a "to do" list, assume that my time and energy are endless.*

7. *If I commit to doing something, it will get done.*
8. *It feels good to be productive.*
9. *I will do my best at anything I undertake.*

Some of the rules that accompanied this were positive. I also remembered that finding the unflattering and revealing rules tucked into my psyche is not reason to beat myself up or "fix myself" so I can be OK. As you said, my way of being is not a disease. In fact, it provides some of my strengths as well as my weaknesses. It's freeing, though, to remember that I made up the rules. If I want, I can change them! Like the rule, "It OK to keep those around me (like my son) less competent so I can feel more competent." Pretty embarrassing.

Within the seminar, we were encouraged to pick one rule we wanted to change. The first step was to "fess up" to the person with whom we had this unspoken "agreement." I did this by explaining to my son what I've been doing (assuming that he couldn't wake himself up for school and work so that I would feel important and useful—but put-upon—when I woke him up). I told him what I was aiming for instead—(he is responsible and I can be more important and useful to him by giving him the power to wake up—or not—by himself. I then asked for his help when he saw me falling back into my old way of being with him. His response was "OK, I have no idea what you're talking about, but that's OK." Which I interpreted as, "You've been to one of your seminars and you're embarrassing me so please don't tell me any more."

So, the conversation was not earth-shattering but something shifted. I realized that I really wasn't helping him by being responsible for waking him up. He also obviously heard more than he was willing to admit because for the first time in 16 years, he's started to hear his alarm clock and get himself up.

My new way of being is "I work with ease." I have created a new set of rules that support this, and although sometimes I still find myself racing the cupcakes to the party, I now can laugh and shake my head and remind myself of my new" way of being."

Crissy started with what seemed to her a small and manageable situation. She has also realized that something big shifted inside during the process. The most exciting part of the shift is still to come. Her son's willingness to get up may seem small (unless you too have been a human alarm clock to your children), but her son's realizing and accepting his responsibility is huge. If he continues and accepts his responsibilities in other areas, he will empower himself to ultimately build a life of his choosing. Crissy's actions, as small as they felt in their inception, will create huge impact if they are continued. The most important result was realizing she had the power to change her world. Once this happens, it usually leads to the next change, and then the next. I find that most acts of empowerment seem small in their inception and then snowball with momentum into a lifestyle that's beyond what we imagined at the beginning.

Crissy's gift wasn't just to herself and her son. His future "partners" have just been freed of a future burden without even realizing they might have had to carry it. By hunting down this seemingly small change in herself, Crissy has touched her son and eased the strain on his future relationships.

Things to Remember In Hunting Yourself Down:

1. **Create a plan that will require new traits that have been hidden.**

2. **This plan should challenge your old "way of being" by taking appropriate risk with new behavior.**

3. **Fear can be an excellent indicator that you are trying new behaviors.**

Step 5: Create Alliances

One of the best tools for staying on track is the creation of alliances. An ally will help you see behaviors that you miss, create solutions you don't see, and keep you on track when you try to avoid.

There are three kinds of alliances that are helpful. The first is an intimate partner whom you trust. This individual must have your best interest at heart and be aware enough to see how you hide. My wife serves this role for me. We have worked through the times we wanted to kill each other and have come to a place of mutual respect. She is also keenly committed to this work because she has seen the quality of our life improve as a result. She has great insight, is not overly concerned with hurting my feelings, and is very inquisitive about how people tick. She also has demonstrated that she is trustworthy as an ally. She doesn't use the material as leverage in other disagreements. She has shown tremendous respect and restraint. She and I have been together for 18 years. This has given her ample opportunity to know my patterns and habits.

The second ally is a mentor. A mentor is someone who has been over the same path you are walking. Once again, an ally needs to be someone without ulterior motive in your change. It follows that this person should be someone who is not a relative, employer, or partner.

A mentor will go over your plans and objectives. He or she will be able to share direct experiences with you about what works and what doesn't. A mentor will be able to save you from making some mistakes that wouldn't be apparent until after you make them.

I hear frequent resistance to having a mentor for two reasons. The first is the awkwardness of requesting someone to serve in this way. Some people have a hard time being served; they feel acute embarrassment at asking anyone for assistance. They feel a need to compensate the mentor in some fashion. They don't understand that many successful people want nothing more than to share their knowledge. There is a strong drive in these people to teach the lessons they have learned along the way.

There *is* one way to repay a mentor. It is also the best way to retain their services. This is to show respect by achieving progress. Show that you value your mentor's time and knowledge by putting it into play. Listening without action will discourage the mentor, and you will lose their participation. I have kept mentors for years by following that one rule.

The third group is a band of hunters. It is a group who are committed to hunting themselves down. They are a source of inspiration, accountability, and insight. They will be able to challenge you to go beyond what you thought your limits were. This book is a product of such a group. For years, I talked about writing without getting to it. My group of hunters was unwilling to put up with my foot-dragging and pushed me past that wall.

To be a worthy group, you need to find a group of peers who are equally committed to change. You may find that some people speak of commitment but won't push past their limits. I think all of us have known someone who was more committed to complaining than to changing. You probably will need to let this person go from your list.

One person who won't move can immobilize a group. He or she can shift the group's focus to what's wrong instead of what's challenging. The inspiration in the group is provided by the challenge of each other's change. When one person moves, the other members have to elevate themselves, or risk falling behind.

The following is an interaction between two members of such a group:

Dear Tom,

I read your "way of being" and was impressed with the courage you showed in really looking at what it was and how it played out in your life. Very honest. I find that I really appreciate what you have to say when you choose to share.

It is amazing how easy it is to see the box that is created when reading other people's way of being and how cloudy it feels when it is my stuff.

Interestingly, I had my way of being challenged yesterday. I was at a cooking class with some colleagues. These are women that were a part of an organization that I belong to. I wish them well but do not have an interest in pursuing a personal relationship. I mentioned to them about planning to make an authentic Ukrainian meal and inviting close friends. To my amazement, they asked if they could join my party!

With gut clenched, I said "Yes." I went home with a headache that lasted all day. So I called them both back and told them it was not going to work for me. It was really hard to do, but I did it. My headache went away. And most of all, I felt a real sense of freedom.

It was a very interesting experience watching those strings pulling tightly and my other ways of being that also bind me kick in.
Lidia

Lidia was caught in the mold of her life. Her friends had invited themselves to dinner and her rule was to comply. With the support of Tom's courage, she was able to change the rule she was living and change her "shape" with those acquaintances. She did it respectfully but firmly.

Lidia had changed her world. The immediate result was the end of a headache and a feeling of relief. I suspect she'd had many headaches from living all those years of compliance.

Finally, I offer a different take on the process, Portia Nelson's poem:

There's a Hole in My Sidewalk
Autobiography in Five Short Chapters
By Portia Nelson

Chapter One
I walk down the street.
There is a deep hole in the sidewalk.

I fall in.
I am lost ... I am helpless ... It isn't my fault.
It takes forever to find a way out.

Chapter Two
I walk down the street.
There is a deep hole in the sidewalk.
I pretend that I don't see it.
I fall in again.
I can't believe I am in this same place.
But, it isn't my fault.
It still takes a long time to get out.

Chapter Three
I walk down the same street.
There is a deep hole in the sidewalk.
I see it is there.
I still fall in ... it's a habit ... but, my eyes are open.
I know where I am.
It is my fault.
I get out immediately.

Chapter Four
I walk down the same street.
There is a deep hole in the sidewalk.
I walk around it.

Chapter Five
I walk down another street.

Change Strategy for Finding Your Freedom

A. Tell the truth about your underlying way of being

    1. Journal about a way of being:
      a) Make a list of your rules
      b) List the rewards for following these rules
      c) List the benefits to how you have lived
      d) List the prices you pay for how you have lived

    2. Keep daily journal of each time you see your rules kept, including:
      a) The situation
      b) The feelings
      c) The results

B. Practice self-acceptance.
    1. Do the split page acceptance exercise from Chapter 8
    2. Keep a journal about parts you struggle with.

C. Clarify intention
    1. What is the new intention?
      a) Not a wish
      b) Not for someone else
      c) Not the same thing in a new disguise
      d) New list of rules to live by —be specific
    2. Simplify life—clear the decks

D. Hunt yourself down
    1. Create a plan to enact new intention
      a) Be specific about people and dates.
      b) Enter into calendar
    2. Challenge old set of rules
    3. Take appropriate risk with new rules

A. Work with a mentor
    1. Someone who has been successful at your task
    2. No ulterior motives
    3. Repay with success

THE FIFTH CHOICE OF FREEDOM

10

Jump: Intention as a Force of Change

"Come to the edge" he said.
They said "We are afraid"
"Come to the edge he said"
They came he pushed them and they flew.

Guillaume Apollinaire

After awareness, what then? Knowing that you may not be who you thought you were is a good beginning to change. If awareness is the *only* thing you have, it is also a good start to a frustrating life. Knowing about your hidden intention alone will no more change your life than knowing about electricity will turn on the lights.

To truly grasp intention you must understand it as a force, not merely as a concept. Just like electricity, if it is treated carelessly or unconsciously it can harm as easily as it can help. Also like electricity, you don't need to understand why electricity works to use the switch.

This can be a tough concept to implement in that most people would prefer to deal with the *thought* of intention, when the real work is in learning to handle it. It would be far more comfortable to sit in a class or read a text where the information is clearly explained and proved. Then, after due consideration and sufficient understanding, the truth would open up insights into ourselves and our deeper nature. This, so we hope, would then allow us to change the desired behaviors. Unfortunately, it doesn't seem to work that way.

Intention is a concept that is best understood through direct experience. In the ordinary life, mastery of intention eludes us, as it is mostly by accident that we have such experiences. When we have those "accidents," the understanding comes from some place deeper inside than the conscious logical mind.

It's almost as if the first step is to surrender control of what we do. Let me explain by example. About 18 years ago, I was walking through a mountain canyon with a friend. We were in the high desert in a long narrow canyon that ran for miles. As we walked, I was keeping an eye on the sky, watching for any buildup of clouds. When we started, the sky was blue and cloudless. After a couple of hours walking, I saw the first big cloud float by, black against the blue summer sky.

Storms in the desert canyons can be tricky. It can rain up canyon and remain bone-dry where you stand. Everything seems fine until you're hit by the flash flood that you never saw coming. When the clouds started to come over the canyon, we turned and started the walk back up to its mouth. We were still a good ways from the end when the rain came.

In the desert, the rains don't start with a few drops and build up to a downpour. It's as if someone opens the spigot and it starts pouring down. We decided that it might be wiser to get out of the bottom of the canyon because the narrow canyon collects water from the surrounding mountains and intensifies the effect of the rain. I picked a spot and started the climb up the steep canyon walls.

After climbing about 30 feet, I found the route I had selected for myself wasn't as easy as it had appeared from the bottom. I was reduced to feeling my way up, searching with my fingers for the next little ledge to pull myself higher. I came to a spot where I was stuck. I couldn't find a way up or the way back down. The rain was making the hold I had tenuous at best.

This is when my mind shifted into hyper-drive. I had always considered myself quite clever. I had gotten through life finding clever solutions that allowed me to ease out of situations that required others time, study, or hard work. Whenever I encountered a really difficult situation, I reverted to what had always worked best—my cleverness. Unfortunately, there is no clever solution to gravity nor could I talk my way out of the peril I was in. I found that I couldn't come up with a solution to being stuck on the cliff.

When absolutely no solution occurred to me, I returned to frantically searching for a way up or down. No luck. The mountain was offering no quick or easy way out. The mind that had always saved me was unable to save me this time.

The reality of my predicament was sinking in fast when I found myself reaching for desperate alternatives. I noticed that there was a thorn bush growing about seven feet from the base of the cliff and almost below me. I started analyzing the risk and reward of jumping for the bush or waiting till I fell, out of control.

I was between a rock and a hard place.

The water was now streaming down the cliff, and as I was hugging it as close as I could, the rain was also streaming into my face and nose. I also was developing a severe case of "sewing machine leg" (where a muscle held in a rigid position for too long begins to shake).

I knew I didn't have much time to make a decision—jump for

the bush and suffer the thorns and likely a broken leg—or worse, or wait until I fell and accept what came from a landing on the rocks. I knew that the bush would be easier, but to make the jump, I would have to leap before my strength gave out. I started to ease off the pack to make the jump easier, when I simply surrendered.

I realized I couldn't make the jump into pain. I refused to accept a choice where I was damned if I jumped and damned if I didn't. My last thought was "I won't do it." Somewhere inside, I realized that I couldn't think my way out of this one. My mind gave up and went blank. I stopped thinking. The tool I had always relied on to protect me had ceased entirely. I was conscious but felt like an observer to what happened next.

I jumped.

Without thinking or even feeling as if I had decided to do it, I jumped. Instead of jumping down, I found that I had jumped *up*. I hadn't even considered doing that when I was trying to *think* a solution to my predicament. It never would have occurred to me because the result would be completely uncertain. Was there a handhold just out of reach? I couldn't have known. I let go of the false security of clinging to a place from which I knew I would fall and took a risk with unknown consequences. My efforts were being directed from a place inside that "knew without thinking." It was so unreasonable, so different to how I lived that I couldn't have done it without first surrendering.

I found a handhold that had been inches beyond my reach. I never would have found it as long as I held on; it was only possible when I jumped. I don't know where the handholds came from. I hadn't thought they had been there a few moments before. I was no longer aware of the fatigue, the rain, or my fear. When I arrived back at the top of the cliff, I felt exhilarated and back in control. I wasn't able to make heads or tails of what had just occurred, except that it was an important moment that I kept to myself because it sounded strange. And I didn't really know how to talk about it. I also felt a little foolish for having been in that predicament in the first place.

On reflecting back, I knew something important had happened, but at the time I was just surprised to be whole. I laughed it off as a "close call" when I joined my friend at the top of the canyon.

At the time, I thought this was a singular occurrence; I have since been surprised by how many people have had a similar experience. The first person I showed this to for the initial editing had an almost identical experience. Upon reading this she wrote back:

That story was awesome. Both because it is what it is, AND because I have almost the exact same story, though I am not sure I have ever told you, at least in detail. This is really freaky; it is so close to yours.

Anyway, when I do tell the mountain tale (because it WAS one of those defining moments), it goes something like this:

I was in the Rockies on a day hike with my brother, who can be rather impatient with my rambling. This day in particular, I was working on a project for a photography class, and stopped often to take pictures.

Exasperated, he went on without me, as it was not a treacherous-appearing mountain, and one that could be climbed mostly upright. As the day got to the middle, I knew I'd have to head back, though I "knew" it would be faster coming down than up, since downhill is always faster— or so I assumed.

What I hadn't accounted for was the loss of shadows, shadows that pointed out the edges of cliffs on my descent down a pathless mountainside.

Over and over, I would spend 20 minutes or so creeping down the side of a rock that looked solid and long from my perspective uphill, only to find myself at the edge of a steep drop-off, at which point I'd have to climb back up to where I started, and try a different route.

After an hour or more of this, I saw this plan wasn't working.

Still confident in my natural hiking and climbing talents and history, I resorted to an old Plan 'B' that had worked well for me in another hike where I had lost my way. I went to where I heard water, and decided to follow the waterfall down the mountain.

I had good associations with this technique, as it carried memories of friends playing in the waterfall, and general silliness, as well as the assuredness that I would be heading in a straight direction downhill. The friends and I had used a waterfall on a warm summer day to work our way down to the bottom of a hilly hike, splashing and playing and congratulating ourselves all the while.

Knowing really nothing of mountains (or even of danger), I had no idea how steep, treacherous and deeply chilling a mountain stream could be—until after I had climbed in it, and was hanging by a slippery rock. I could go neither up nor down, nor even sideways at this point, and suddenly knew without a doubt that I could die here.

I heard a whimper escape my throat, and the last coherent thought I remember was of being aware that I had two choices—I could whimper until I lost my slippery grip and go crashing down the rocks to almost certain death, or I would have to do something, though I had no idea what. The next thing I saw was my foot above my hand, in an impossible position, and then I was up and out.

Being so freaked out by the waterfall at this point, I used the sound of the water as a guide to GET AWAY from it, and that alone led me in a consistent direction, and I eventually found a path. Overjoyed at this unexpected find, I had barely taken a few steps when the sun dropped the rest of the way behind the mountain, and I was in total darkness.

Knowing it was not safe to move far in any direction, I wondered if I could survive a night where I knew the temperature dropped drastically, even in summer. I had come too close to death to stop and let it overtake me now. I gathered my wits again, pulled out my camera flash unit, fired it once in the direction of the path, and continued on down the mountain in baby steps, flashing every few feet. My flash battery died just as I saw the lights from the village below, close enough now that my brother could help guide me the rest of the way with his shouts.

When I was finally in front of him, I broke down, relieved and angry at his leaving me up there - but mostly grateful—for what I could only later explain as "maybe adrenaline?" that put my foot unconsciously in a position I could not normally reach."

As I have shared the story with others, I find that we are not the only ones to have such experiences. There seems to be a common thread to the stories. First, the reality sets in that there is no escape, no going back. Second comes the understanding that solving this problem the way you have solved things in the past won't work. Third, there is a sense of urgency created by danger or desire.

Over the years, I have heard many stories that were similar, stories of people who have accomplished extraordinary feats when faced with dire consequences. It is most common for us to have this experience by accident. (I don't suggest that anyone try to create such a situation on purpose just to test themselves.) If this were just an ability to save ourselves from accidental death it would be interesting, but not useful in other situations. It is when the same ability shows up in other situations that it gets interesting.

The most important thing to understand is that the ability we're speaking of is the ability to "will" or "intend" our lives to be different. Strangely, this isn't a conscious willing but a will that shows up only after we surrender conscious control. It is as if the most dynamic and powerful tool in our mental arsenal is unavailable to us until we need it most and get our normal thinking process out of the way.

In the first six chapters, intention showed up as an ability to create a way we would live. We saw how decisions, made at an unconscious level, affected peoples' lives in many ways. Here, intention shows up also as an unconscious but very creative response to danger. What would happen if the response could become conscious? What if we could have some measure of control over this incredibly powerful ability?

I have noticed this ability has found its way into other areas of my life. What I hadn't noticed was the connection between them. There have been a series of events where I have accessed a force of will to create change. In Chapter 6, we saw this force of will being used to establish long-term directions for life through "ways of being." In the desert, this force of will came out in response to danger. It will also show up in support of a cause.

The dreams or causes that trigger access to this force are those we feel are bigger than ourselves. I, as well as some of the people I have interviewed, have realized that we have used this same strength to make our dreams come true. The dreams I refer to here are not personal self-serving ambitions, but causes that are above and beyond our personal desires. These are beliefs that we hold so passionately that we would sacrifice ourselves for their sake.

In fact, to have such a cause is to sacrifice a part of you. The sacrifice certainly entails giving up your time and the other pursuits you could enjoy during that time—your hobbies, sleep, friends, job, and family time. When you are really committed, you may also find yourself giving up your limits. You find yourself overcoming fears that had held you back throughout your life, fears that you had struggled with for your own sake without success but now seem to ignore for something that seems bigger than you.

I have seen this frequently in situations as diverse as when shy people convert to a religion that asks for evangelism, and they find the ability to overcome their shyness to evangelize (often reverting immediately to shyness upon completion of the mission). I have seen this when people become part of a team and suddenly find themselves working with a diligence and effort that they have never applied to their own needs. My friend Kate had a perfect example from her youth. Remember—she had always described herself as invisible, never wanting to stand out and or be noticed.

After my first year of college, I found myself in the unlikely summer job of door-to-door encyclopedia sales. This was not a job an "invisible" person would choose, but their advertisement had me believing I would be making a guaranteed high weekly salary for "giving away" books to "qualified" families. I believed in books, and figured I could give up being "shy" to travel the state and give books away to those who needed them. By the time I learned that I was actually supposed to knock on doors and SELL encyclopedias, I had spent two weeks in "free" training, had made no money, and had turned down my one other job option (in New York) for the summer.

Predictably, I was worse than bad at selling; after another week of making absolutely no money, and a night where I came very close to being raped by the boss, I had had enough and quit. I sat at home, stewing over being a miserable failure for the first time in my life. This skill seemed like it SHOULD be learnable; though nearly everyone in my training class had dropped out by now, it appeared that at least a few people were successful—how else could the company stay in business?

After about a week of this, I learned the "jerk" boss had been fired, and a manager with a good track record had been brought in from North Carolina. I decided to give it another try, since I had no other prospects and wouldn't be able to return to school if I had no money. The new boss was an odd-looking man named Randy Ariail, and he took me on as a "project." He went with me that night to watch what I was doing so he could find out what wasn't working. As before, I did the three-hour presentation nearly word-for-word as I had been taught, but left empty-handed. Randy later pulled me aside and said, "Look, the only difference between you and these people who ARE making money at this is that you're a little bit smarter than they are." He also told me that my problem was in not knowing how to "close" a sale. The next night, I watched him work, and as he predicted, I got to see him actually make the sale. The night following that, I made my first encyclopedia sale. I was elated.

After that, I did better. Knocking on doors never did get easier, though. But because it only took one sale a week to make the money I needed to return to school, I was quite content with one, sometimes two, sales per week, after which I would take it easy. Randy was not a particularly high-pressure boss and was more concerned with our well-being than our sales. He would sometimes take us to his house, where his wife would feed us before he would drop us off to start knocking. Occasionally, he would even take us to a movie first. He seemed to relish his role as "coach" for all of us, and wanted nothing more than for us to succeed. He even offered to co-sign my loan for my first car, when my father refused to do so. He intervened for me when the car salesman had obviously taken advantage of my lack of experience. And when I wrecked the car after only two weeks, he stayed on the auto shop to speed them up. We all learned many things from Randy, most of which had nothing to do with encyclopedias.

Coming from a small Indiana town, I hadn't realized how naïve I was. In Randy, I had found both a protector and a mentor. He was someone who could teach me many things about life that I desperately wanted to know. And unlike the earlier sleaze-ball boss, I had no concerns about being taken advantage of. I don't think I was even aware of the strength of the loyalty that this inspired.

One week, the "Big Boss" (VP of the encyclopedia company) came to town to see what could be done to make our crew more productive. Randy was under the gun and feared for his own job, so I was inspired to set to work to make him look good. That week,

I not only broke my own record by selling FOUR sets, but also outsold everyone else in all 50 states! Of course, Randy was beaming, the VP left town satisfied, and I immediately went back to making one or two sales per week. I was a bit startled to learn that they all (including Randy) had assumed I had finally "hit my stride" and would now maintain that level of success. I had only done it so Randy would still have his job. In my view, the crisis had passed for now, and I had no motivation to work that hard for any other reason.

I remember when my own career was just beginning. I was 21 and had very little experience outside of school. I was working for a company that produced seminars. Being a recent graduate, I was convinced of the life-changing effects of the work we were doing. To me, this was more than a dream job—it was the ultimate form of service to humanity.

At the time, I felt uniquely *un*equipped to do the job. I was responsible for enrolling participants in the seminars. This required both sales and organizational skills, neither one of which I seemed to possess. It was my responsibility to fill the class with 20 new students each month. I was so excited about the seminar that I was sure everyone would want to come. The first month, we had eight people. When the facilitator arrived and asked me what happened to the 20 I promised, I told him I had done my best and next month we would have 20.

At that time, my "best" meant that I did everything I could within the limits I had placed on myself as a person. I took a very "reasonable" approach to what I was capable of and had clear ideas of where my boundaries were. I knew I wasn't a very good salesperson, and I acted just like that.

When the next month came, the 20 people I promised turned out to be 10. Once again, I had promised to do my best. I felt like I was changing slowly and getting better at what I was doing. This still seemed good enough the next month, when my 20 people turned out to be 12. I was showing steady progress and this seemed reasonable to me. Over the next six months I never reached 20 people. I then moved on to learning the facilitation side. This seemed more in keeping with my natural inclinations, and I was happy to get away from responsibilities I didn't enjoy.

Two years later, I found myself once again tasked with the responsibility of enrolling people into a seminar. I was in a different city with a different seminar company, but had the same boss as two years previous. I had an agreement to enroll 15 people in this new seminar that he would be coming in to facilitate. I had been working at it non-stop for 30 days and, on the morning of the seminar, I had 12 people ready to go.

My boss was flying in from San Francisco to L.A. the morning of the seminar. I called him at 7:00 a.m. to arrange to pick him up. He asked how many students I had enrolled, and when I told him 12 people, he said he wouldn't come. It seems he remembered two years before how I had constantly promised a result that I didn't deliver.

This time, he was committed to keeping our agreement. He felt that if he didn't take a stand for me that I wouldn't either. I told him that he was being unreasonable, and he agreed. He said that I always had a good reason for not doing what I said I would do, but that he would no longer support me in my reasons. Then he said I had three hours to complete my end of the agreement.

I told him that I had given it everything I had for 30 days; how could I possibly complete in one morning what I couldn't do in a month? "I don't know," he said, and also said that it was my problem, and with that, he hung up

At the time, I was angry with him. I thought he was being inconsiderate, unreasonable, and a jerk. I didn't know what to do. I was thinking about calling those 12 people and telling them we were canceling. Then I realized I would have to tell them why. Some very reasonable excuses occurred to me that would sound plausible but I couldn't do it. I felt like I was letting them down and, more importantly, I was letting down the dream.

At that point, I had a feeling well up inside me. It was a feeling of "I can't let this happen." I took out the phone list of prospects and started calling the people who had said "no" just the day before. Nothing had changed from the previous day except one thing. Their excuses were the same (they also had less time to arrange for time away from work or family), but I was different. I didn't know anything more and my skills were the same, but my intention was different.

For three hours, I was more committed to achieving my dream than I was to living inside my limits. At 10:00 when the facilitator arrived, there were 15 people in the room. I hadn't given away the business through discounted prices or special deals. I had been completely committed to achieving my goal.

Afterwards, I felt both exhilarated and relieved. The feeling of exhilaration lasted for quite a while, and I noticed that I had little trouble achieving my other goals. I also found that I liked the process of having my boundaries stretched. I spent the next several years looking for opportunities to work with that boss, because I knew he would push me to be more than what I saw in myself.

What I had discovered was the secret to seeing something greater in myself. What I had yet to learn was how to enjoy not only the outcome of going outside my comfort zone, but also to enjoy the feeling of being out there.

At first freedom felt uncomfortable. I felt out of sorts, it felt too vulnerable and exposed. I thought people were staring, as if they knew or could see something was different. Freedom didn't feel the way I had dreamed it would. In time, it felt exhilarating. I felt elated when I was able to break through barriers that had been confining to me. Each time I tried something new, it led to a greater conviction that I really could have what I wanted.

Surrender

The common themes in all the stories where intention reared its head were these: The simultaneous feeling of "I will not allow this" occurred just before "surrender." There are, embedded in my three stories, the keys to achieving this remarkable experience. Let's go back over the moments and see what they can tell us.

My first experience of "I will not allow this" was the moment I described in the earlier chapter when I guaranteed that I would never lose control of my emotions. It wasn't a consciously thought-out decision, but came completely unbidden by my conscious mind. Notice that this wasn't "I don't like this," or "I don't want this." It was "I can't allow this." The first two statements are common to children. They are expressions of dislike, with an overtone of powerlessness.

Clearly, I had been boiling under the surface for some time and had been unable or unwilling to express my frustration. This kind of defiance was not in my vocabulary at the time. I was taught to honor and respect my parents. That, coupled with the love I felt for them, made it very difficult for me to find the words to express such difficult feelings; I had to surrender control to let them out at all. When the feelings finally came out, there was so much pressure built up under the surface that I made a promise that came to direct my actions for years. As you have probably noticed, surrendering control is not something many of us do well, especially in areas that feel important to us.

The downside of using the power of intention in an unconscious manner is the price to be paid. The most obvious price in this instance was losing access to my feelings; the other price was that the unconscious strategy didn't work. There is a flaw that I often see materialize when people make broad sweeping promises like the one I made. They almost always backfire. It is much like the character in Walt Disney's animated version of *The Magician's Apprentice*. He takes the magician's wand and uses it to animate the mops and buckets to magically clean the floor. Unfortunately, he doesn't know how to stop what he started. The apprentice was trying to get out of cleaning up a mess and ended up with a much larger one. He did this by using forces that were beyond his understanding, and once the genie was out of the bottle, there was no way to stop it.

So it was for me. I had used an incredible force to clean up a mess. The mess was not being able to say how I really felt about how I was being treated. It doesn't matter that I was young, didn't know how, or had never been taught. It seems unfair that we have to learn such hard lessons, especially at such tender ages. It really doesn't matter if it's fair or not. The reality is that we get to learn about intention at some point, and the lesson may be painful.

As to how my plan backfired, I think the best analogy is the volcano. The earth can only hold so much pressure before it blows. That's how it was with me. My promise to not have such big feelings didn't mean they did not *happen*, only that I didn't *feel* them. Life is full of situations that cause frustration, pain, and anger. I had decided that feeling them was dangerous; what I discovered was that not feeling them was even more so.

Whenever enough pressure would build up, I would blow up. It didn't happen often, but when it did it was ugly and entirely surprising, especially to me. I would suddenly find myself reacting in inappropriate and frightening ways without a moment's thought. This would often be in response to provocation, and therefore seemed justified, though not to *that* extent. Afterwards, I would return to calm for the next few years until the pressure would build again, and once more, without warning, I would find myself doing something stupid and regrettable. That was how my intention backfired.

The same was true for Nancy, the woman from earlier chapters who had decided to be "nice." Her rules led her to try to make everyone happy. She ended up making some of the most important people in her life upset by her inability to stand up for herself. All too often, I see that people who have used intention in such a way find that the promise they made hasn't worked out in the end.

My second experience of "I will not allow this" was when I was stuck on the cliff and faced with injury or death and was unable to stomach the apparent choices. That same feeling came up inside, it's as if at some deep place inside a part of me screams "NO! I will not let this happen!" There were also no clear acceptable choices within my normal abilities. This necessitated the need to surrender the state of mind that determined my normal abilities.

The third instance was in working with my unreasonable boss, but in support of a cause. Once again, I found myself faced with an outcome that I would not tolerate. Again, I had no discernable solution, and again, the only way out was to let go of what I knew. You may have noticed by now that each time I "surrendered," I was really giving up my limitations.

Surrendering My Comfort Zone

Like most functioning adults, I have spent years learning how to cope with most of the normal situations in life. I have figured out how to get by using the gifts and abilities I was born with to earn a living, be a partner in marriage, and handle the other responsibilities of life. I do this in a way that is consistent and familiar; in other words, I operate within my comfort zone. This isn't a bad thing, nor is it something that needs to be changed just for its own sake.

I am convinced that the larger part of human ingenuity and inventiveness has been employed to make our lives more comfortable. It is normal and natural for us to seek ways to save time, effort, and energy, and to avoid stress. Operating in one's comfort zone serves us in that way. Spending most of my life in ways that are familiar and comfortable isn't a problem; it is the point where I am *unable* to operate outside my comfort zone that I find problematic. One solution is to make sure that I never need to. To achieve this would mean that I always took the safest path in every situation; I would have to make sure that I never took any risk. There are people who do just this and seem satisfied with the result. I find that I get bored when I don't try new things. I also find that there are dreams I have that require me to take risks if I am to fulfill them. I am not a proponent of taking risks just for the thrill of it; I find that I will take big risks only when they are in the direction of my dreams.

Herein lies the dilemma. Each time I enter a new or risky situation, I try to do things the way I have always done them, without even thinking about it. I will find the most comfortable way to accomplish the new goal by trying what's familiar. Many times in trying my normal style, I will find a way to succeed. I do this even when it is harder than learning something new. This is true in simple, non-threatening areas, as well as those that scare me to death.

I remember, for instance, learning to play tennis. My backhand was poor and felt unnatural, so I would run around the ball to hit it forehand. This meant that I missed a lot of shots, but at least I felt I was on familiar ground. It wasn't until I couldn't stand losing that I started to hit with the backhand. It never did feel natural until I found an even "better" solution; I quit playing tennis.

This has often been the pattern of my life. I will do what's most comfortable. When I am required to try something too difficult in a task that doesn't have much meaning, I will find something else to do. This works fine until I am faced with something I can't do without. This is the secret to learning to use intention.

"I don't ask someone if they want a million dollars; I ask them if they can live without it." My friend, Ron Rosselot, heard Coach Lou Holtz say those words during a speech. When Ron brought them to my attention, I realized that in these words was the key to when I have moved past my limits to use the power of intention.

When I consider all the things I want or daydream of having, the list is enormous. I will have those things as long as I can achieve them using the comfortable style that I have developed over time. If achieving that thing becomes too challenging, I will try to find a clever solution to getting it. If that fails, instead of changing how I go about getting things, I move on to the next thing on the list. If you were to ask me if I wanted a million dollars, I would say 'Yes!' If you were to examine whether I was living a life that would lead to a million dollars you would see that I am not. I would take it if it came my way, but I won't do *whatever it takes* to have it; it's not my *intention* to be a millionaire. I can live without it, and so I have.

When I consider the things I can't live without, the list is rather short. These are the things I truly value in life—things I would do anything to achieve. I would like to be able to say that the list is longer because there are so many things I think I should value so highly. The truth is that I may pay lip service to a great many things, but I don't really follow them up with "can't live without it" action—I only do what's comfortable.

I have an ideal picture of what I should be like. I "should" exercise daily, watch what I eat, take care of the environment, always tell the truth, meditate, and pray each day, be helpful to the needy and sick, be more attentive to my friends, write more letters, help out more around the house ... the list goes on and on. These are things that I feel I should do better. I will do a little work with each, but the truth is that I don't feel the urgency of "*I can't live without it.*" Thinking I "should" do more may motivate me to do some; I will put some effort into them. I won't really commit to "whatever it takes" unless my intention shifts and I realize I have to have it.

When I consider what I truly haven't been able to live without, I can tell what's on the list by the effort I've given and the risks I've taken. I can tell I'm committed to my life by the risk I took in the story of the mountains. I know I'm committed to my work because I have consistently risked my limits to achieve dreams that I feel are much bigger that I am. I see that I am committed to my marriage in that I have risked opening myself and challenging the "way of being" that has been comfortable since I was a child. Anytime I'm willing to surrender my limitations, I know I'm committed.

Having the commitment to do whatever it takes is the first step in learning to use the power of intention. Until you can honestly say, "I can't live without this," you will never find the freedom to be as great as your potential; you will never be able to live up to your greatest dreams. You will always stop a little short; you will pull up just short of surrendering your comfort.

When I say "comfort zone" I don't mean "pleasant zone." You may be thinking that you aren't operating in your comfort zone because parts of your life don't feel very rewarding, or seem very enjoyable. Many people live lives that are unpleasant and stick with them for years. They may have an unpleasant job, one that they dislike or aren't suited for. They may have an unpleasant relationship, one that is dull, lifeless, or outright abusive. Unpleasant, as bad as that may sound, is attractive for some in that it can be comfortable in its safety. It may be painful, but the fear of taking a risk often seems so much worse.

When I am teaching and tell groups about this step (to surrender), I usually hear one of two responses. One is "I don't know what I really want." Some people have lived a life without ever really discovering what they are passionate about. In fact, many people find only after losing something—their partner, health, career, or time itself—that they realize those feelings of "I can't live without this" were hidden in them and only revealed in loss. I suspect that they were somehow protecting themselves from the risk they would feel compelled to take if they ever caught on to what they really wanted. One way to stay safe is to never admit that you want anything that would require any risk. Not admitting that, even to yourself, doesn't make it go away; it only makes you blind to what you need to do to get or keep what you really want.

The second response I hear is "There is something I want but it's not as if I can't live without it. I will still be alive if I don't get it. Life will go on; I may regret it a little but I will get over it." *"Can't live without it"* may, on occasion, mean that you would die without it; more often it means that you will suffer the slow death of losing your vitality and the joy that comes from living a life filled with passion. Hiding in the literal meaning of words may seem clever in the moment, but it is really just another way to stay comfortable, a way to forgo the threat of giving up control and surrendering. Living in the spirit of those words "I can't live without it" will take you past your limits and allow you to fulfill what is greatest in you.

Between A Rock and a Hard Spot

Most people I talk to have spent their lives making sure they stay out of a spot like that. When I get excited about the possibilities of not only being in that spot but being there *on purpose*, people tell me I'm nuts. Who would want to be in an inescapable dilemma? Their resistance gets me all the more excited because I know this is the next step to surrendering to the power of intention. Here is how it works:

Saying, "*I can't live without it*" is the level of commitment required to elevate you to achieve beyond your norm. That commitment is *the rock* in being between a rock and a hard spot. You can think of that commitment as an agreement. When you say, "I can't live without it," that is an agreement that you will do whatever it takes—no matter how difficult or unreasonable—to fulfill your obligation. You may feel you have made this deal between you and another person, you and God, or solely with yourself.

One of the most decisive factors in whether you will keep your agreement will be in how "reasonable" you are. Let me explain. Today millions of people will make a commitment. Some of these commitments will seem trivial, while others will seem like things they can't live without.

When the average person makes a commitment, they add an unspoken addendum of "if it's reasonable or convenient." This is how it works: They say, "I'll meet you at 6:00." What they mean is "I'll meet you at 6:00 (if it's reasonable or convenient)." This is reasonable because unforeseen circumstances may occur that make it difficult to do the things we say we will do.

When someone breaks an agreement with us, they will often blame it on an excuse. Before offering us the excuse, they will check to make sure that it is plausible; in other words, is it a *good enough* and *likely enough* reason to not keep their agreement. When they deliver the excuse, they are actually offering us this in place of the result they have promised. We then examine the excuse for its reasonability. If we believe that the excuse is *reasonable enough*, we then accept it in place of the promised result. This is what I term being between a rock and a soft spot. They are committed to doing something hard but find it easier to create reasons than to create results.

Imagine for a moment that I loaned you $10,000, which you agree to pay back next Thursday. Things get tough, the $10,000 is hard to come by, and you start to question your ability to produce it by Thursday. Since you are a reasonable person, you start to prepare all of the reasons why the $10,000 result is impossible. You figure that it is easier to convince me that I shouldn't get my money back than it is to create the $10,000. You think you are between a rock and a soft place—if your excuse is *good enough* (for example, I lost my job, I was sick, etc.), then I will be soft.

This creates a situation that reinforces powerlessness in people. They get in the habit of finding excuses, and eventually they come to believe they are incapable of achieving results, and then they actually can't. Having made an agreement, many people will *unconsciously* decide between producing an agreeable excuse or producing the result to which they've actually agreed.

If you borrowed that same $10,000 from the mafia, you would probably think a lot harder about what was easier. You know that the loan shark isn't going to be a soft spot. You know you are truly between a rock and a hard spot. In fact, you may decide that it is easier to produce the result you agreed to instead of ever offering an excuse.

When you commit to something big, that is the rock; whatever holds you accountable is the hard spot. If you think that you can soften that spot with reasons, you probably will try. The true genius of allowing yourself to be between a rock and a hard spot is that you may realize that your limits are the soft spot. It may finally occur to you that overcoming your self-limiting beliefs is the *only* solution to the fix you're in.

When Michael Avery, my boss from the story of enrolling people in seminars, first employed me, he was willing to accept my reasons. In time, he decided he wouldn't do that any more; he decided that he wouldn't dis-empower me by arguing with me or acknowledging my supposed weakness or incapability. I had the power to do what I said I would do. When he decided to hold me accountable, I found I had the will. I then understood it would be easier to keep my agreement than it would be to get him to accept an excuse. It became easier for me to overcome my limits than it was to get that particular rock to move.

As for the mountain example, there was never any question about it. I couldn't talk my way out of falling or talk the rocks into cushioning my fall. The only alternative to disaster was to overcome my boundaries. Gradually, it has become clear to me that to access intention, I *needed* to be between a rock and a hard place. In order to step up to a level of ability that was beyond my normal limits, I had to know that I could not live without my dream and that the way to get it was to surrender to the greatness within.

This isn't just a story about me. I have described this process to many people over the last several years. When I meet someone whose dreams seem to them to be bigger than their ability, I do my best to put them between that rock and a hard place. The following is a story that happened last year. I met a woman named Sue who was on the same path I had been on many years before. Like me, she was dedicated to fulfilling her dream of helping people change their lives. She had also come to the place where she had employed all the usual means that were within her comfort zone and had come up short:

I took a self-empowerment course that changed my life. I had done a fair amount of self-discovery work before I entered this seminar, but the techniques and format of this course guided me to results I had not been able to create before. It helped me integrate many bits of information into an understanding that allowed me to start living more of the life that I desired. I was so impressed by the course, it's power, and it's alignment to my personal beliefs that the answers lie within us and not in anyone or anything else, that I became very involved in a variety of capacities with the organization, eventually becoming a city director.

A new class was being proposed by our advanced seminar facilitator (Steve Sherwood, author of this book) that centered on connecting to the greater unlimited source within ourselves. I became very excited about adding this class to our repertoire because it is rare to find a series of classes that move through the protective layers we put around ourselves and open a path to our true essence and then really spend time exploring and celebrating that. I had found classes working on personality/ego or blocks, or on essence, but rarely a series that did it this well.[1] I was passionate about making this available to as many people as possible.

The board approved the new class but there was turmoil within the organization, including opposition to this new offering. I was put solely in charge of making this new seminar happen. I had three participants from the start that were committed to go and six weeks to get to the necessary ten. This is a relatively short time to build a class; usually there was three-four months to book students, and that is for a proven seminar. During that time, I used all my usual techniques and knowledge to fill the class. As I approached my deadline and didn't have any more students and no solid prospects, I cancelled it.

After having done so, I realized that I couldn't live with that

---

[1] See http://www.Lifesuccessseminars.com for more information.

decision. I discovered that in canceling it I was expressing my limitations and not my potential.

So much of life gets spent on what's missing and isn't right in our lives, I knew we must include more on what is complete and whole in us, our essence! I wanted to work in an organization that was directly promoting this focus. I felt strongly about the balance and impact it could have. Miracles happen by tapping into this realm of pure potentiality. I got to experience it as I connected to that piece within me that refused limitation.

I reassessed what I had really been up to during the six weeks:

- *I had allowed my focus to be distracted by others and their perspectives. I had done what I have done all my life and that was to let other people's view of me define me and influence my behavior in an attempt to feel safe (I couldn't be more than they said; that would mean people would expect things from me) and, in a round-a-bout way, to please them by not challenging their views; they get to be "right."*

- *I felt I had held to my personal values but (I now realized) only to the degree that I was comfortable; I abandoned my values when I felt at risk. I totally violated the value I truly hold most dear. I had allowed fear to run the show, while I said I treasured love as the greatest gift we can ever give ourselves or share with another.*

- *I believe in my strong connection to my own inner source but I question myself and become subservient to authority figures if I feel they must (or should) know more. I must maintain my "good girl" status and not offend those I need to love me. In doing so, I was dishonoring myself. I could trace this to EXACTLY how I behaved in my family. I gave up my inner knowledge if it meant it didn't match what I was told by my parents. I couldn't take the risk of putting myself before them. The cost throughout my life has been very high.*

- *I allowed my focus to get tied up in the "stories" other people told me instead of helping them to create what they said they wanted. I was creating what I intended, which was to mirror people's limited expectations of me and not rock the boat. In doing that, I was enabling them to do the same. Upon inspection, this was EVERYWHERE in my life...anywhere I had a limitation that said "you can't have that," or "you can't have a salary like that," or "you can't afford a vacation like that," I was truly mired in the "stories"—not in the possibilities.*

When I realized I had been focusing on what I didn't want instead of what I did want, I asked to put the class back on the schedule. I now had only three days to get the seven participants I needed that I couldn't get in six weeks before.

I remembered the story you had told me about being held to your word of having 15 students in a class and you only had 12, and in three hours you got the other three students. Inspired by the story, proving it was possible, I set my intention that NOTHING else was acceptable.

Everything that had been going on during the turmoil was a reflection of some part of myself that was in turmoil. I judged myself, I underestimated myself, and I allowed the minutia to distract me from the bigger picture. When I decided those parts of me could exist but didn't have to have my attention, I adjusted my focus to what I now truly wanted to create, which was this class. It was like being in a room with a whiny child that is looking for all the attention for the bad behavior, while the gentle, patient child waits calmly, undemanding of your attention. I found this going on in my mind, the constant chatter juxtaposed next to a centered calm, the tornado versus its still center. Quite simply, it was a matter of choice. With the new focus, creativity flowed, and when I contacted people about the class, there was an openness and interest and people started signing up...,by 4:00 on the third day I *had my ten participants, and ended up with 15. The class was an interesting and amazing success.*

What else I learned from the situation: all experiences in life are gifts for me to see myself more clearly and to give me the option to choose new possibilities in how to handle a situation. The ONLY reason I ever get upset with another person is because they are challenging me to step up in a way I don't want to or am afraid to, don't feel I am ready to, or feel like I already have and don't want to do it again. That's it. It's not about the other person or the situation...it's always about ME.

I had heard all these realizations before and had some level of "mind understanding" of them, but I had not truly decided to live them; I pretended to myself and others that my life was all about supporting these principles, but I only did so up to the edge of feeling safe.

Sue had discovered the secret to unleashing the power within. She had felt the squeeze of being between the rock and the hard spot and had let the pressure crack away her limits and free her to be great. She had done so because she had taken a stand for a cause she couldn't live without. I find it exciting that Sue has now gone on to tackle even bigger dreams; she is in the process of selling her home and business and moving to Hawaii to pursue her life-long passion of working with dolphins.

Think about your life for a moment. When was that time that you found yourself in an untenable position and then saw yourself doing something so out of character that you can't believe it was *you* who did it? I imagine many of you have had a moment or two like that in your lives, one of those shining moments when you surrendered and went beyond your boundaries and jumped into the unknown, jumped without thinking about what the outcome would be, jumped while being guided only by the power of your intention. When you jumped, you found a genius and strength inside that carried you toward that which you couldn't live without.

It is an important step in helping people with accountability to place them between a rock and a hard spot, until what is holding them accountable is that they "know that they can't live without it." You may find this extremely challenging or feel that it is outside your character to be the hard spot in someone else's life. You may have to challenge the rules you have about how you live in order to give someone the gift of not accepting their excuses. Even though it may seem unkind, it is a blessing as long as you are objective and your motives are purely in their interest.

You may have found that spot without help, as Lidia did. Lidia had found her way between a rock and a hard spot. After 16 years of marriage, she knew hers would never be a fulfilling one. She was stuck in her own way, just as I was stuck on that ledge. She had the choice to continue grasping to a life that would never meet her needs or to jump into the unknown. Here is her story:

Between Trapezes by Lidia Young

When I decided to end my marriage of 16 years to my childhood sweetheart, I knew I faced a major crossroad in my life. As a stay-at-home Mom for 12 years with two daughters, I also feared how joint custody would impact my self-perception, in addition to how I would spend my time.

I knew I had to get a job and find a way to support myself. I felt insecure. I had been out of the professional arena since my children were born. Even though after college I had an exceptionally satisfying professional life as a social worker and community leader, it seemed like eons ago. I did not feel my skills would be in demand. I had decided to leave my former profession to take care of my kids a dozen years earlier. I chose to be a homemaker while my husband climbed the corporate ladder. As a result of his promotions, we moved to new cities every year. In yet again a new location, I had no professional contacts.

I had thoroughly enjoyed the gift of being a mother—my art and my work at the time. I remember an experience in Wal-Mart as the court date approached when the reality of what I had chosen set in. I saw a young mom with a beautiful, barefoot toddler in a shopping cart and felt a huge pang of longing and terror. I felt envy for the seeming security of their lives. I also experienced the pure fear of not knowing what would come next. In that moment, given the chance, I would have gladly traded places with that mother.

Here I was at the same impasse I experienced many times before. The terror raging in my head said I was crazy to give up my financial security. After all, I lived in a lovely, new home on a golf course and had all the comforts that I wanted. Not only that, had I not made a commitment to my family that I should continue to honor? Maybe I should try one more time to make my marriage work. Perhaps all the other attempts to try to resuscitate my relationship were not a real indicator of the capacity of the union. Lost in indecision, I took a deep breath. When I got quiet, I could feel what was in the deepest part of my heart. I already knew the truth. For me the marriage was over and no amount of additional time would fix that. I could go back, but I would very soon face this dilemma again with the same result. I realized that being afraid did not mean it was the wrong decision, only a hard one. I knew I was facing the most difficult challenge of my adult life. Walking out of the store, I fought the impulse to continue second-guessing myself.

Even though terrified and insecure, I decided to look at the want ads. Nothing seemed to match my previous work history, but one listing jumped off the page. An outdoor challenge adventure organization searched for facilitators. I had no knowledge about ropes courses, but I applied anyway and got the job. It started a new chapter in my own journey of self-discovery.

My boss, a generous teacher, willingly shared his knowledge with his staff, and I soaked up what he offered. He proved to be an important mentor. Being on the ropes course helped me remember how much I loved working with people. I experienced the satisfaction of helping participants see the connection between how they behaved on the challenge course and how they lived their lives. I was reawakening to a part of myself that I truly enjoyed.

During my year on the job, I decided to go to graduate school and become a clinical social worker. At the University of Kansas, I met a teacher who hugely impacted my perspective and who went on to be my clinical mentor. During the years of supervision with him, I honed my instincts and went beyond theories. I learned to trust myself. I built a thriving counseling practice where I worked with individuals, couples, and families for ten years. I also co-facilitated a support group for people with HIV+ and AIDS for eight years.

My career has now taken another major turn. I have significantly reduced my clinical practice. Most of my week is devoted to being an executive coach for individuals and working with leadership teams in the corporate setting. It is exciting to help leaders become more effective in their professional and personal lives.

Had someone told me—as I stood in Wal-Mart watching that mother and child—that I would have such a satisfying life now, I would not have believed it. I have the best balance of all possible worlds—a richly rewarding professional life, deeply honoring relationships with my amazing adult daughters, and a truly intimate marriage with my husband of eight years. Had I not risked jumping into the terrifying unknown, I would have missed the precious life I am so deeply and gratefully living.

After years of trying to fix her marriage, or fix herself to be satisfied in her marriage, Lidia finally knew there was something she couldn't live without. She now knew she couldn't live without a relationship that was supportive and nurturing to her soul. She had tried to solve her crisis in the easiest and most comfortable ways, but had come to understand the real meaning of "I can't live without it."

When I was stuck on the ledge, I knew that I had only a few

minutes before I either had to jump or fall. Lidia had the added burden of time. You may have thought of extra time as a blessing, but too often it just allows us to fool ourselves as to how critical the choice in front of us is. The decisiveness that comes from urgency seems like a hardship when it happens but is often a blessing in hindsight.

Lidia's marriage was probably already over; it had died, but she hadn't been willing to admit it. It is like the story of the optimistic window washer. He had fallen off the top of the empire state building in New York City. When he passed the 56th floor, he was heard saying "So far so good." That is often the way it is when we have too much time to make important decisions. We make choices that have us plunging to our imminent destruction, all the while thinking we have more time. Lidia's marriage had fallen years before; it just hadn't hit the ground yet. As long as you have enough time to consider the possibilities, you also have time to pretend that you can live without taking action.

The real advantage of having the time is that you can use it to clarify your intention. Take the time to figure out what you really can't live without, so that when you jump you aren't just jumping away from a bad situation, but are jumping toward your real heart's desire. I have witnessed too many people who have taken a leap away from a bad situation only to find they leapt into a new one just as bad. They left one abusive partner to find another abusive partner, or they left one unsatisfying job for another that ends up feeling the same. The importance of doing the work in the first eight chapters is that it allows you to realign your intention so that when you make the leap, you are jumping toward something that will truly be different and new. Until your underlying *intention* changes, your attempts to change—no matter how noble in appearance—will always take you back to where you started.

When Lidia jumped, she grabbed hold of a new direction for her life. She didn't find the same type of husband as the one she had been with, nor did she replay the same kind of relationship. She also found a new direction for her career. She has, in the last few years, realigned her intention away from "I must fit in" and the rules she lived by. Think back to the child of Ukrainian immigrants from Chapter 5.

These were her rules:
1. Listen carefully before speaking.
2. Being different isn't acceptable.
3. If you want to change things, go slowly and get consensus.
4. Be cautious in dress and mannerisms.
5. Don't challenge the status quo.
6. Be careful not to offend.
7. Don't let people know if you're smarter than they are.
8. Let others take the lead.

Lidia has taken her listening abilities, her respect and appreciation of people's differences and found in herself the abilities of challenging authority, taking appropriate risk, and a way to tactfully address very divisive issues in corporate teams. I am in touch with her—here is an excerpt of her most recent letter:

Tuesday I facilitated a five-hour session with a fortune 500 company. I was working with 50 directors and managers while three VPs observed from the back of the room. They gave me permission to explore the impacts of the last three reorganizations (three sets of massive layoffs since January). Most of the people in the room have had to lay off 50% of their staff (with no reduction in work load). It was especially a watershed moment for me because at the start, one of their internal trainers, who was also observing, said that I would not be able to get these very burned-out people to engage. I told her I wanted to start with a model of change, which included stages of grief, and she said they have had so much of that info that people would be bored. She said I would embarrass myself and that she was only trying to help. (It did not feel she was very supportive or helpful!) It was such a cool moment. I felt alone but in a great way because I knew the work was NOT the cognitive info and that I would be able to respond to the group no matter what their reaction. I was not all attached to the info I brought, so even if they would have complained "old stuff," I would have invited them to choose the point of focus.

I thanked this trainer for her opinion and then said I trusted what I was about to do. I knew where I wanted to start and where I wanted to end—with them feeling heard and like they did have power. And I did it. It was an amazing day. They engaged in a huge way and did not hold back. It was probably uncomfortable at midpoint for the VPs because of the feelings coming to the surface, and it was so cool because the VPs hung in and ultimately saw that ,with the right facilitation, you can address tough issues and come out the other side in a much better place.

The group felt honored and heard and by the end of the day was ready to focus on being excited about the next day (with the in-house trainer) when they were going to redesign their departments, etc., and focus on doing their best, even in very uncertain times. AND they felt a great new bond with each other. They now had permission to talk about the issues and reach out to each other. It was exciting for me because this was a group I had not worked with before, so they were all strangers and still they elected to engage in a big way.

After the session, a couple of the VPs suggested that maybe I could come and work with their groups. Many of the participants said the session was unlike anything they had experienced in their many years at work there (one person said their 20+ years) and that it was greatly needed.

So, I am ready for more and know I am well equipped to do this work.

Lidia obviously has changed the rules she lives by.

Had she started the process by attempting to change only her rules without mastering the first five steps, she would have let her unconscious intention shape that new set of behaviors to guide her back to her old familiar results.

Lidia had escaped the limits of her old self-image. She had fallen, like Houdini, against the door of the "escape-proof prison" to find that the jailor had forgotten to lock the cell. She was free—free to explore the limits of the gifts and creativity she was born with. She has jumped out of comfort and into a future that is unknowable and from which there is no return to the safety of her familiar life.

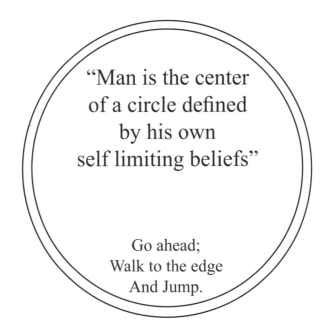

"Man is the center
of a circle defined
by his own
self limiting beliefs"

Go ahead;
Walk to the edge
And Jump.

About the Author

Steve Sherwood has earned a national reputation as a facilitator of experiential training programs. He specializes in helping people grasp the underlying motives behind their behavior—be they productive or unconstructive. His students commonly realize welcome breakthroughs in their careers and personal lives.

Sherwood has managed a variety of training organizations and sales teams. And he has designed and facilitated experiential education programs for the travel industry, health care, and consumer products. He coaches executives and CEOs who are involved in career transitions.

Steve Sherwood developed the "Unleashing the Leader Within" seminar in conjunction with Witmer & Associates. It is one of the most powerful and inspirational seminars available in the United States. The "Unleashing" experience allows business executives to understand and manage their true strengths and limitations. It is a root-cause look at what enables people to achieve by capitalizing on their successes while avoiding the pitfalls of their limitations.

Sherwood provides seminars in three areas:

Professional Development Series
Benefiting business owners, managers, and executives in formulating strategic leadership in their organization or desirous of taking that next critical step in their career.

Personal Enrichment Series

Geared toward people who believe they can create their life, or have been waiting for the chance to make the change of a lifetime.

Facilitator Training

Is for those who are interested in learning how to inspire others and in changing their lives by developing and teaching their own seminars.

Steve lives in Macon, Georgia with his wife, Lisa. Together they import and restore antique furniture.

To learn more about the author go to

www.stevesherwood.net

For Additional Copies of

Finding Freedom

Use the form below or go to:
www.CincyBooks.com

Cincinnati Book Publishers
2449 Fairview Avenue
Cincinnati, OH 45219

PLEASE SEND ME _____ *COPIES of* Finding Freedom

MY CHECK FOR _____ IS ENCLOSED.
PLEASE MAKE CHECK PAYABLE TO: Cincinnati Book Publishers

1-9 COPIES $23.95 + $1.56 TAX (Ohio) + $1.99 S&H = $27.50 EA.
10-50 COPIES $20.00 + $1.30 TAX (Ohio) + $.1.00 S&H = 22.30 EA.
50+ COPIES- email info@cincybooks.com

NAME

ADDRESS

CITY   STATE   ZIP

PHONE   EMAIL

VISA   MASTERCARD   DISCOVER   AMERICAN EXPRESS
(CIRCLE ONE)

CARD #   EX DATE

NAME ON CARD

THANK YOU!